Airedale Terrier Training
Dog Training With The

No BRAINER Dog TRAINER
"We Make it That Easy"

How to EASILY Train Your Airedale Terrier

By Paul Allen Pearce

PAUL ALLEN PEARCE
PUBLISHING

Copyright © 2015 Paul Allen Pearce

Introduction

The motivation for this guide came when my brother Tom and I were recently reminded of what it is like to bring your first dog home. This occurred when a first time dog owner, in all of her excitement and anticipation, bombarded us with a barrage of questions about preparation and how to begin training. We hear these often, but then I realized that inside my successful "Think Like a Dog" breed specific dog training series I had left room to elaborate on puppies first days, insight into early potential puppy issues, and to add more information about canine behavior. Listening to this new dog owner, Tom and I were motivated to compile some essential information to help these first-time trainers and newbie dog owners, and of course, the more experienced, while keeping the command training section in an easy to understand instructional. Then I added three additional commands, *release*, *touch*, and *learn names* that I placed into the Bonus Tricks section.

This book now includes a *"new puppy"* section written especially for the new dog owner, which includes instruction for the beginner trainer and owner. Tom added some information that he thought one should have in place before bringing a puppy home. A compilation of commonly made mistakes gleaned from research and experience, also made its way into this guide.

The first section of this book prepares new dog owners for the addition of a puppy to a home. This includes instruction on the pre-arrival preparation of your home, and a list of the numerous puppy items that should be gathered in anticipation of the new arrival. Additionally within this section there are important points regarding your mental preparation, as well as some other elements that you should consider as a new dog owner.

The second section was written specifically to educate dog owners on the training processes and methods needed for success in the behavioral shaping of your new companion. Contained within both the first and second sections, are facts about typical puppy behaviors highlighted to help you anticipate your puppy's needs, as well as to explain some of his mannerisms and idiosyncrasies. These sections also serve to explain the mental requirements, as well as the actual tangible tools needed to undertake responsible ownership and training of your puppy. Inside is an important and thorough explanation of *socialization* that explains why it is essential to puppies throughout their lifetime. Both of these sections are packed full of useful, easy to understand information in support of your success as a new dog owner.

The third section contains instruction on command training, in which you will be led, step-by-step, in the use of the highly effective rewards based clicker training.

The final section explains the basic cares, needs and requirements of your new companion. You will find detailed instruction and information on basic grooming, nutrition, as well as some owner based goals recommended for you to work on while caring for your dog.

Inside this guide, I'm certain you will find complete and concise training support featuring highly useful information culled from years of personal training experience, other professional trainers, various training manuals, research, and years of experience living with my canine friends.

Though this guide approaches training as a serious endeavor, your dog will teach you otherwise. In an attempt to keep this book lighthearted, I have infused my dogs' playful spirits throughout this instructional by adding some humor and fun throughout.

By obtaining this training guide today, you will be well on your way to acquiring the necessary tools and knowledge to assure your success as a dog owner, and trainer.

I am confident that you will find this guide informative, easy to follow *and fun*.

Now, move onto to Chapter 1 - "Puppy Up!" - And begin your joy-filled journey of puppy ownership and training.

The Airedale Terrier
(Waterside Terrier, Bingley Terrier)

Posing an aristocratic profile, confident, and assertive personality, and armed with a quirky lovable face and unkempt coat, owning an Airedale is an adventurous undertaking that pays highly. They love being close with their families, are flexible to rural or urban living environments, capable of many tasks, and have a friendly cheerful personality. You will find them extremely loyal to their family and quite entertaining.

Versatile and athletic this courageous medium sized dog competes in agility, conformation, hunting and field, obedience, and rally. Other uses include guard, watch, rodent control, and military/police work. They need open spaces, and at least a medium sized backyard, so it is not suggested for apartment living. A medium size yard is good, but they also need a lot of daily exercise including long daily walks, runs, swims, and games such as retrieval work. As the largest of the terrier breeds, they have been anointed the moniker "King of Terriers".

Airedale's make a fine family dog, including a kinship towards other dogs in the family. As usual, it all comes down to being properly socialized and trained. This breed exhibits good intelligence, independence, and can be a bit stubborn in its temperament during training, a common terrier trait, but over-all is a quick and capable learner capable of performing many types of work and sports. They rarely bark, and if they do, it will be for a good reason.

History

Originating in Yorkshire England by the River Aire, and bred to hunt Otters and other small game such as otters, ducks, weasels, foxes, badgers, and rats. They were bred by working class people trying to improve upon the dogs already available to them, where as many other terriers were bred by aristocracy. Their genesis took place in the 19th century around the area of Airedale England. Originally, the Airedale was known as the Bingley or Waterside terrier. To make the Aire a better swimmer a mixture of keen eye sighted and nosed hunting terriers were used in combination with the Otter Hound resulting in a bigger and improved swimming and hunting terrier. Highlights are its keen eyesight, hearing, bravery, and intelligence.

Airedale's have been used in working, hunting, and herding, and further used in Africa, India, and Canada to hunt big game. They enjoy a good chase of animals, so they must be trained very well if they are to be used in herding, otherwise they may irritate the livestock. They are one of the first breeds used for police duty in Germany and the United Kingdom.

During wartime, especially in WWI, this breed was used for messenger duty, sentry duty, searching for wounded soldiers, running telephone cables, and carrying carrier pigeons. It has been estimated that over three-thousand Airedales lost their lives during wartime.

They were first shown in 1864 England, and recognized by the Kennel Club in 1886. The Airedale Terrier was recognized by the American Kennel Club in 1888. In two-thousand and fifteen, they are ranked the fifty-sixth most popular breed registered with the AKC.

Health

Like humans, dogs have the potential to develop ailments and diseases. Many of these ailments and diseases vary in type and prevalence, from breed to breed. Consider this fact when picking out your new puppy, and beware of any breeder that makes a claim that the puppies of their particular breed are *"100% healthy."* A reputable and honest breeder should know and share any health related issues that the breed you are purchasing or inquiring about might have, or that could potentially surface.

They are a tough and healthy breed, with only a few potentially major ailments, such as eye, heart, hip issues (hip dysplasia), and hypothyroidism. Keep an eye on their skin and if it is overly dry, add Omega-6 and Omega-3 fatty acids to their diets. They live an average lifespan of 10-12 years. Cancer, urology, and old age are the top three causes of death in the Airedale breed.

Consult the CHIC database and your countries Airedale club for further in depth health information about what is being done to solve these issues.

Prior to acquiring your dog of choice, I recommend reading about canine health related issues and common breed specific ailments. By familiarizing yourself with the signs and symptoms of a potential disease or sickness, you will be empowered to be the first line of defense in support of your dog's health and wellbeing. By completing routine physical examinations of your dog, frequent fecal inspections, as well as recognizing any gastrointestinal problems, all helps to assure optimal health of your companion. By observing and understanding your dog's healthy behaviors and regular patterns, you will easily be able to identify when your dog is not feeling well, and to deduce if medical attention is needed.

In your position and role as alpha, you are responsible for providing the best possible care for your dog, assuring his or her wellbeing and comfort. Do not hesitate to consult your veterinarian if you observe your dog displaying peculiar behaviors or showing any signs of discomfort. It is very important to maintain your dog's scheduled exams, mandatory check up's and vaccination appointments. Uphold this duty, so that your dog can enjoy the vitality of good health that he or she deserves, and is entitled to.

Long daily walks are recommended for maintaining a healthy dog, regardless of the breed. Walks can be opportunities to practice leash training, socialization, and aid to the over-all mental and physical wellbeing of your dog.

Besides daily long walks, Airedale Terriers require at least one hour per day of varied types of exercise, whether this is achieved through play, games or sports. Tracking games are a great source of exercise and mental stimulation for Aire's and when grown they can accompany you jogging or cycling. The first two years of an Airedales life will require that they be provided additional exercise for them to be calm at night and not be restless in the house, where they are active dogs.

Loneliness and boredom are enemies of the Aire. I advise that you always provide your new puppy with plenty of toys to keep boredom at bay and to reduce the chance of potential destructive negative behaviors from overtaking their naturally sweet disposition.

Feeding Your Airedale Terrier

Age, weight, and activity levels are a few of the factors that can change the food requirements of your Aire. Once you have determined the appropriate amount to provide, feed an accurately measured portion, at regular times, to help maintain their optimal weight. If you wish to feed your dog a raw food diet or a mix, please do your research and consult your veterinarian prior to any adjustments to their meals. Be sure to keep plenty of fresh, clean water available for your dog, and it is considered a good hygienic practice to clean your dog's bowl after each feeding.

More in "Nutrition"

Proactive Measures for Puppy Selection

If you want to buy an Airedale Terrier puppy, be sure to find a reputable Airedale Terrier breeder who will provide proof of health clearances for both of the puppy's parents. Health clearances are official documents that prove a dog has been tested for, and cleared of any, or all breed specific conditions, however a clearance does not guarantee against acquired diseases or congenital abnormalities. Remember, even under the best breeding practices and proactive care measures, puppies can still develop diseases.

For the Airedale Terrier breed, you should expect to see a health clearance from the Orthopedic Foundation for Animals (OFA) for hip dysplasia, as well as a clearance from the Canine Eye Registry Foundation (CERF), certifying that the eyes are healthy. You can also confirm health clearances by checking the OFA web site. For more information, refer to the club website, breeder, or veterinarian. Consult the CHIC database for other tests and their schedules.

The Orthopedic Foundation for Animals (OFA www.offa.org) maintains an open registry with evaluations of hips, elbows, eyes, thyroid, cardio, and additional canine health issues. They also provide clear definitions of the test categories to help you understand the grading system. PennHIP (www.pennhip.org) is another registry that tests and evaluates dog's hips.

The American Kennel Club (AKC) conducts large canine research studies on diseases that affect purebred dogs. Their health program is under the direction of the Canine Health Foundation (CHF), and is in partnership with OFA, and additionally does breed testing and provides a centralized canine health database called, the Canine Health Information Center (CHIC). The results of these tests are maintained in a registry, and dogs that have completed all of the required exams, including testing of the hips, elbows, and eyes, receive a CHIC number. Along with the breed-testing program, there is the CHIC DNA Repository. CHIC is trying to gather and store breed DNA samples for canine disease research. The goal is to facilitate future research aimed at reducing the incidence of inherited diseases in dogs. You can search the database to find out if a specific dog has information listed about it. More information about CHIC is available here: http://www.caninehealthinfo.org

To be accepted into the CHIC database, breeders must agree to have all test results published. This enables the reader to see both good and bad results of the testing. Obtaining a CHIC number does not imply that the dog received good or passing evaluation scores. The CHIC registration also does not signify as proof of the absence of disease, and all information must be read and evaluated. CHIC allows the information collected to be readily available to anyone with an inquiry.

Care

You are responsible for the welfare of your new puppy or dog. Please treat him or her with respect and love, and this will be reciprocated tenfold. Dogs have been human companions for thousands of years, and they are living beings complete with feelings, emotions and the need for attachment. Before bringing home a new dog or puppy, please determine if you are capable and willing to provide all the needs that your new family member requires.

From the time you bring your pup home, positive training is a great start to introducing your new pack member to your household. You should be aware and sensitive to the fact that dogs have an amazing capacity for memory and recollection of those experiences. With this in mind, please refrain from harsh training tactics that may intimidate your puppy and that potentially can negatively affect personality or demeanor. When you train your new puppy, give him or her the respect they deserve, and utilize all available positive reinforcements. The result of your positive, proactive training methods and behavior modifications will be that your dog's abilities, traits, and characteristics that are buried within the genetic profile of their specific breed, will shine. I am an advocate for beginning with rewards based clicker training, followed by vocal and physical cues for your young dog to learn to become obedient to commands.

Crate training has positive benefits, and provides a safe place for your dog to nap, or simply to be alone. In addition, crate training at a young age will help your dog accept confinement if he ever needs to be transported, boarded or hospitalized.

Appropriate, early, and ongoing socialization will help you and your Aire throughout his or her lifetime. Expose your new puppy or dog to a wide variety of situations, people, and other animals. This helps to prevent shyness, aggressiveness, possessiveness, and many other potential behavioral problems, meanwhile supporting the bond between the two of you. Remember never leave young children unsupervised around dogs or puppies. Also, be aware that situations of aggression may happen no matter how loving, gentle, and well trained a dog may be.

A routine care program is essential for any dog, and should always include basic hygienic practices. For the optimal health of your pet, scheduled care should include the care of the coat, nails and teeth. It is important to get instruction from your veterinarian for the proper cleaning method of the outer and inner ear.

The Aire come in tan with black or gold with black, always with a slightly curly, rough topcoat and softer undercoat and usually appearing unkempt. For grooming, the hair should be plucked twice yearly and if kept stripped they will shed little to no hair. They do require a bit of extra grooming to keep their beards and coat free from burrs, food, and drink, use this time as an opportunity to practice handling, inspect for ticks, fleas, lumps, or rashes. To keep their coat in top condition use a slicker brush a couple of times per week.

Airedale's naturally have a longer tail, but in the U.S., a few days after birth most have their tails shortened for show purposes. The U.K. does not allow this type of alteration.

Training

As with most hunting terriers they possess a strong prey drive that can translate into single-minded pursuit and independent thought, after all, hunters have to think and strategize. Aire's can certainly display this attitude and they cannot control their inherent genetic markers. Though at times it can be frustrating, these dogs are by no means regularly disobedient unless they have not been socialized and trained properly. This strong prey drive that cannot be trained away, which is why it is vital that your

Airedale responds quickly to the *leave it, stay,* and *come* commands. If they spy some prey they will give chase.

Keep them occupied with physical and mental challenges, and a sharp eye out for any jumping issues, and respond to jumping behaviors quickly, showing your dog that jumping on humans is unacceptable. When out walking and playing with your dog only allow off leash when they are in safely enclosed areas.

They are rather easy to train after you have garnered their respect as their leader. You should enjoy training and have an obedient dog by following the guidelines for rewards based training, remaining consistent in all things Aire related.

Gradually begin socializing your puppy from the time you bring him or her home. Proper early socialization that continues throughout your puppy's lifetime will provide you with a well-adjusted dog that is able to handle almost any situation in a calm manner. Early, thorough, and continual socialization is important for your Airedale Terrier. You do not want your dog being territorial and wary of strangers, so it is important to expose them early to a variety of situations, animals, people, and places. Socialization benefits you and your dog by providing you both with peace of mind. With good socialization, you can expose your Airedale Terrier to different situations with the assurance that he or she will look to you for guidance in rules of etiquette for the indoor and outdoor world. Socialization is the foundation for all well-adjusted dogs throughout their lifetimes.

An effective incentive is to make everything you do seem fun. Always refrain from forcing your puppy to do anything they do not want to do. Highly prized treats are usually a great incentive to do something, and you will find that a fun, pleasant, friendly, happy, vocal tone combined with the treats will be ample reward for good behaviors and command compliance. Begin training all new commands indoors. This includes silencing all of your audio-visual devices that act as distractions to dog's sensitive ears.

Training should always be an enjoyable bonding time between you and your dog. Remember that all dogs are different, and that there is no set time limit for when your dog should learn, understand, and properly obey commands. Always have fun during training, remembering to keep your training sessions short, and stop if either of you are tired or distracted. I always suggest beginning training new tricks or commands in an area of least distraction. I promote starting with rewards based clicker training and ending with vocal and or physical cues for your dog to follow.

If you notice any negative behavioral issues, and are not quite sure if you are offering your dog proper socialization and necessary training, do not hesitate to enter your puppy into a puppy kindergarten class to assist you with training and socialization. Behavioral issues do not have to be present to enroll your dog into a puppy kindergarten; this assistance will benefit the both of you. Properly research the available classes so that their approach matches your own. The time to enroll your puppy is usually around eight to ten weeks of age, and after their first round of shots, although some kindergarten classes will not accept puppies until they are three to four months of age.

Reward good behaviors, but do not reward for being cute, sweet, loveable, or huggable. If you wish to reward your dog, always reward after you issue a command and your dog obeys the command. During your training sessions, be sure to mix it up, add a variety of toys and treats, and do not forget to have fun. Remember to provide them with ample daily exercise to keep them fit, healthy, and to keep behavioral problems at away. Provide consistent structure, firm authority, rule enforcement, love and affection, and you will have one heck of a dog for you and your family.

Look Inside!

Get Your

Free

New Dog Training Jump Start Guide!

Learn How Your Dog Really listens and Communicates with other dogs and YOU!

"Save-Massive-Time" Training Like a Real Pro!

Included Free

Table of Contents

Puppy Up!	1
Common Mistakes First Time Dog Owners Make	3
Preparing for Your Airedale Terrier	10
Puppy Proof Home Protocol	10
Puppy Training Prep	19
TRAINING EDUCATION	26
Unconditional Socialization	26
Separation Anxiety	35
Handling Training	47
Clicker Training	56
Training Pointers	65
Solving Unwanted Behaviors	70
Rewards in Lieu of Punishment	74
Everything Treats	76
About Alpha Dog's	82
Terrier Breeds Traits	86
BEGIN TRAINING	93
Housetraining	93
Teething, Bones and Chew-toys	97
Clicker Response Training	106
Name Recognition	109
"Sit"	112
"Come"	114

"Drop it"	122
"Leave it"	127
"Down"	130
"Stay"	133
Leash Training	138
"Go"	150
Jumping is a NO-NO	154
Barking	159
Nipping & Biting	167
Digging Help	172
BASIC CARE	178
Dog Nutrition	184
The End is Only the Beginning	201
3 BONUS TRICKS	204
DON'T THiNK – BE, ALPHA DOG	221
Airedale Terrier Facts	222
About the Author	227
Other Books	229

Puppy Up!
How to Use This Training Guide

First, take the time to read the entire guide, so that you can familiarize yourself in a general manner with the methods and instruction contained within. To avoid feeling overwhelmed from the density of information contained within this guide, pace yourself during your first reading. After your initial read, keep it nearby so that you can easily reference it as needed. Having the guide handy at all times, will help to keep the information and instruction fresh in your mind. Just as your dog requires ongoing training practice, you as the owner and trainer need to remain sharp on the training points, processes and methods. It is important for you, as the commander and chief, to maintain a focus on the goals and outcomes of the training.

- While following the training steps, let your dog learn and proceed at his own pace, as there is no set timeline to advance to subsequent steps contained inside each training section. Do not rush to the next step because *you* are ready; make the decision to move forward based on your dog's obedience of the commands, or compliance to the requested actions.
- If you are on a training step and you realize your dog is not ready to have advanced, back up a step and repeat practicing over a few training sessions. Then proceed to the next after your dog is performing the current step successfully at a proficient level.
- Always remain alert to the possibility of your dog feeling weary or having a low concentration day. If you are, stop the session and return to it at another time.

- Always remain attentive to the possibility that *YOU* may be feeling weary, having a low concentration day, or are in a bad mood. If you are experiencing any of these signs, do not start the training session, and simply wait until your status improves.
- If your puppy is not progressing, or appears not to be hearing your commands, you should consider a visit to your veterinarian. It possible that a problem with your dog's hearing, sight, or a medical condition is impeding his training.
- If you are using treats in your training, and your dog has recently eaten, *do not train*. His full stomach will reduce the effectiveness of the intended reinforcement of the food rewards. Wait at least two hours after feeding to improve the effectiveness of the treats.
- Because training can sometimes be very taxing on you and your dog, and at times your dog will push your buttons, never let him know that you are angry, or at your limits. Remember, it is always of great importance to maintain a light heartedness, and use plenty of laughter, during training

Be sure to download the free *New Dog Starter Guide* that contains my *Bark Charts* to assist you in staying organized while you track your dog's progress. Up to date notes make it easy to track exactly which part of training your dog has successfully accomplished, and which needs more work. Downloading the **FREE** New Dog Starter Guide dog-training support materials not only provides you immediately useful information, but also is a gateway to other free training materials. Enjoy your training.

Common Mistakes First Time Dog Owners Make

If you have previously owned dogs, then you probably recognize some of these potential mistakes. If this is your first time bringing a dog into your family, then being aware and prepared of the most common mistakes made by first time dog owners is your best means of identifying and preventing these issues *before* they surface. Below is a short overview of some things to watch out. This is not a complete list, but meant for awareness of some potential major issues that you can thwart by becoming self-aware that you are not accidentally falling into any of these negative thought processes. This training guide will delve deeper into these topics with further explanation and detail on how to tackle them.

"It's a lot more work than I expected. Owning a dog isn't what I thought it would be. "

Many first time dog owners will confess that they were unprepared for the burden of responsibility that comes with dog ownership. Most people who acquire a dog are often uninformed and frequently ill prepared to have a dog under their care. There is a romantic notion that comes with the idea of keeping a dog; it's all playful romps on the beach, delightful trots down sidewalks and trails, games of throw and fetch in the park, automatic obedience, all effortless, simple, intuitive, and low-maintenance relationship with man's best friend. While some of these things can become a reality, this idealistic, romantic notion has certainly caused many dogs, and their humans, unnecessary misery and heartache.

The reality of dog ownership is it consists of great responsibility and commitment. When you have chosen to adopt a puppy, you have signed an unseen contract obliging you to a lifetime of care for an animal that looks to you for leadership. You will assume the role as the *alpha*, and for the wellbeing of your new companion, you must follow through with all of the responsibilities that comes with this important position.

"My dog is untrainable; he will not listen or obey anything that I say."

Dogs thrive under clear, well-defined rules, issued under confident, unwavering leadership. Guidelines and directions need to be well structured and consistent. By establishing a distinct set of rules for your dog to learn and follow, paired with consistent obedience enforcement, you will turn out an easier to train, well behaved, and relaxed dog. By following a regular daily schedule for walking, feeding, training, and play, your dog will surely flourish. Being in charge does not mean that you have to be overtly physical, hostile, or excessively vocal. Remain firm but reasonable in your administration and enforcement of the rules established. As pack leader, your dog will look to you for cues and direction. To be an effective superior you must always project yourself with steadfast confidence, and it is essential that you maintain continuity in your guidance. Within the processes of training your dog, the consistency of your teaching and the uniformity of your rule enforcement will firmly establish *you as the alpha*.

"There is definitely a communication problem between my dog and I."

This is a common issue frequently reported by first time dog owners. Identifying the signals within the behavioral displays of your dog will help clue you into his needs. By reading your dog's body language and other subtle cues in his manner, you will be empowered to resolve what appears to be issues of miscommunication. This miscommunication often manifests during housetraining. If your dog continues to relieve himself indoors, then maybe you are not identifying the signals that he displays which indicates his need to relieve himself. First, you need to pay close attention to your puppy, so keep him within view, observing for signals that should cue you to his needs. Sniffing the floor, revisiting a previous relief spot, circling, looking at, or walking towards the door are certain indicators he is in need of a potty break. Eventually, you will begin to recognize your dog's signals of communication. With a proactive attitude, combined with a sensitivity to the unspoken needs of your companion, your response time to his needs will certainly improve over time.

A couple of things to ask yourself is, *"Have I taught my dog what I am trying to communicate?"*, or *"Has he learned the command or rule yet?"* Just because you completed a couple of training sessions does not necessarily mean that your dog has retained the command you are issuing, or even understood what you were attempting to teach. Make sure to follow through with your training, and remember not to demand something from your dog that he has not been given a chance to learn yet.

"My dog is a wilding and he is riddled with behavioral issues."

It is common for first time dog owners to find themselves with a juvenile dog afflicted with a multitude of behavioral problems. Negative behavioral issues manifest themselves in various ways, such as jumping up on people, aggression, possessiveness, excessive barking, playing rough, biting, and growling or snapping when commands are issued. Each of these behaviors stems from a historic lack of rule enforcement and incomplete training during the puppy's developmental years. Lenient owners who frequently gave in to their dogs when challenged, or owners who were permissive, letting their dogs run amuck, are common causes of poor behaviors in adulthood.

Often, because early in life these dogs are poorly supervised and trained, they appear seemingly uncontrollable. The poor beasts who have the misfortune to grow up without structure are regularly given away, put into shelters, or even sometimes euthanized. This can be avoided by remaining proactive in your dog's development through implementing proper methods of training, becoming well versed in canine behaviors, and becoming intimately familiar with your dog's various patterns of communication. Early, consistent rule establishment and enforcement is imperative. The time you invest in observation of your dog will have high returns. In addition, your willingness and diligence in understanding and cataloguing his various expressions, is value added. The most important question to ask yourself, prior to dog ownership, is *do you have enough time and patience to train and properly care for a puppy?* If yes, then it is up to you to provide unconditional love, patience, guidance, and structure immediately upon the arrival of your new addition to the family. These are the basic essentials any new dog owner should have available in their toolbox in order to assure that the puppy can grow into an obedient, well adjusted, and *wanted* dog. Whether this is your first or tenth dog, if the proper commitment is made, owners and their canine companions can live a life of harmony with a mutual understanding that the human retains the power as commander and chief.

"I will treat my dog like a human child."

That is not going to work, and you and your dog are doomed to failure if you begin your relationship with this approach. Yes, your dog is a living, feeling creature that certainly deserves all of the love and respect that we humans can offer them, but remember that your dog is a completely different species, and his care should reflect this fact. Dogs have instinctual behaviors, including barking, digging, marking, chewing and more. All of these attributes serve them well in the wild, but as a domesticated pet, these things certainly need shaping and curbing. As everyone is well aware, dogs can be aggressive and will bite if provoked. This often inflicts injury on those in harm's way. Biting is a behavior, that if not nipped in the bud early in life, can cause dangerous problems in the future.

The behavioral modifications to shape and steer a dog will be much different from that utilized in the training and upbringing of a human child. Even though it might be tempting to personify your cute little pup, it is a serious mistake to treat dogs as humans. A dog's body language and vocalizations are quite different from a human, and if you try to interpret their actions from a human perspective, then there will likely be a lot of misinterpretation, resulting in frustration and mishandling. Approaching your dog as a human can lead to all sorts of problematic communication issues, and create fertile grounds for negative behaviors to grow from. For you and your dog's sake, you should make a concerted effort to learn about dog communication and behavior, maintaining a species-specific sensitivity, thereby assuring continuity in communication. With this respected, you will be empowered to form a healthier and happier relationship, that you will continue throughout the lifetime of your dog.

"My puppy is acting as a fur covered wrecking ball that is destroying my house!"

Yep, that is normal puppy behavior. Your puppy is getting to know his environment and the objects that occupy it. His curiosity usually entails tearing into any object that he can sink his teeth into, meanwhile discovering the joy of tearing out the stuffing from inside your slippers and sofa cushions. You can simply chalk this up as normal puppy behavior.

A few tricks exist that can help keep your items intact. Prior to delivering your puppy home, you must puppy proof your home by removing all objects from the floors and in areas where your puppy might gain access. Be sure to utilize his crate or baby-gate when you are away from home, and your puppy is left alone. You can also take these measures when you are both together at home, and you need him out from under foot. It is also an essential tactic to provide him with a plethora of chew toys to discover, gnaw and occupy his time. Taking these measures, as well teaching your puppy that his toys are the only things that he is allowed to put in his mouth, will positively shape his behavior, and garner your eventual trust. As your puppy gains your trust, you can reward him by granting him further access to the house.

"I will train my puppy when I have time."

That statement reveals an undesirable recipe to have an unruly, out of control puppy who knows no rules or boundaries, and I poorly equipped to act appropriately in various situations. Owning and training a puppy requires an ongoing and consistent commitment of your time and energy. Immediately after bringing your puppy home, you have to begin investing time into establishment and enforcement of rules, thereby giving your puppy a chance to gain your trust. Daily, weekly, and monthly schedules for puppy activity and training, paired with effectual socialization requires regular time spent with your puppy. None of this is optional. If you neglect investing time in your new companion, you will likely end up with an uncontrollable puppy that in order to train in obedience, and train out unwanted, negative behaviors will likely require some serious hands-on-work from a professional.

"I will choose a dog based upon their looks."

Although looks are to be considered, it should not be the singular factor in making the decision. There are many factors to consider when choosing a dog for you and your family. Breed traits, personality, grooming, health, trainability, indoor or outdoor, and much more. New dog owners first need to know that they have the time necessary to train and care for a new dog or there is no reason to continue. It is unfair to bring a dog into an uncaring environment. Afterward they must diagram their schedules and choose a breed that best fits the family's lifestyle, likes, and dislikes. Armed with that information you can begin reviewing breeds that fit well with your family lifestyle and research further. Then after narrowing your search begin to find a reputable breeder. Selecting a dog breed that fits correctly with your lifestyle will begin the process of having a successful, prolonged, dog-human relationship. Start today by acquiring more free information about puppies.

Preparing for Your Airedale Terrier Puppy Proof Home Protocol

You have selected your puppy, and you are excited that finally the day has come that you are bringing your new puppy home. A second of panic occurs as you wonder, "Do I have everything my new puppy needs?" I do not want you to have those thoughts, and fortunately, there are plenty of resources to help. I have put together a small list of items that everyone needs to have in their home and car before bringing a new furry creature into their home.

Puppy proofing your home entails removing all harmful items that a puppy might chew or swallow, unfortunately, that means everything. Puppies love to put anything into their mouths. After all, they are kids learning about the world. It will be necessary to elevate electrical cords, remove floor debris, and all other random objects that a puppy can chew, eat, or swallow. Thoroughly inspect your entire house that is accessible to your puppy. Apply bitter spray to appropriate furniture and fixed objects that require protection. Take extra caution removing from puppy reach all chemicals, pharmaceuticals, and other toxic liquids that might be accessed around the house.

Baby gates can be used to quarantine areas away your puppy. Not Bill Gates baby, but gates that keep babies out of trouble. Avoid any accordion type gating system because they can cause harm to your puppy. Make sure the gates fasten securely and are structurally sound. Stairs and workrooms should be blocked in addition to any other rooms that your new puppy should not be allowed.

BEWARE! Puppies will investigate anything new and easily accessible. It is *time to change habits.* From the time your puppy is coming home you can no longer walk in and carelessly place anything onto the floor. This includes your backpacks, groceries, clothes, briefcases, containers, handbags, leashes, collars, plastic or paper bags, and all other objects or clothing that you normally toss carefree onto the floor. Your home is a landscape that needs to remain puppy proof. *Train your mind* to be puppy proof. Anything accidently dropped or spilled must be immediately retrieved or cleaned from the floor.

"What do I need to do to make my home ready for a new puppy?"

1. *Read a complete puppy care book* about your Airedale Terrier *prior* to bringing your puppy home.
2. A correct sized *crate*. Your puppy will be spending quite a bit of time in its crate and it should be comfortable and sized appropriately for your puppy.

Your puppy should be able to stand up, lie down, and turn around in the crate but not much more, because it will make it more likely that your puppy will have an accident inside the crate. Add something soft and washable for him or her to sleep on. Thoroughly clean any messes that occur inside the crate. Try diligently to avoid crate accidents. Your puppy's crate will be used for sleeping and resting and the sooner he is used to it, the better.

3. *Playpen* made from wire or wood. Wire pens can be configured into varying sizes and shape, but wood are limited to four sides and a fixed sized wall. Avoid accordion style walls.
4. *Chew toys* of varying kinds. Be aware of the size and durability. You need durable toys because most puppies will try to tear them apart. Note that some breeds puppies can destroy almost any type of toy, and that all are able to swallow balls larger than their jaws. Nylabones™, rubber balls, tough squeaky toys, and rawhide are desirable.
5. *Collar* and *leash*. Choose an appropriate sized collar and style for your puppy. A good idea is a wide, flat, buckle type collar that can be expanded as they grow. Your puppy will be growing astonishingly fast for the first few months. Your puppy is small, so select a lightweight leash that is about six feet (2meters) in length. Begin introducing your puppy to wearing their collar and introducing the leash before venturing outdoors. Your puppy can sport the expensive designer collar after they are grown.
6. *ID tags.* Regular tag with contact information, or one that is electronically chipped.
7. *Puppy food* that is recommended by your breeder or veterinarian. Use only high quality foods without bi-

products and artificial additives. If you are interested, research and consult experts about raw foods diets. Raw food diets provide a healthy alternative or addition to puppy foods.
8. *Food bowls*. Stainless steel bowls retain less bacteria than glass or plastic.
9. *Puppy proof spray* to apply to items that you do not want your puppy chewing. Sprays that humans cannot smell but are bitter to puppies and keeps their mouths off furniture and other items. Bitter apple is a common spray.
10. Potty accident cleaner. *Enzyme cleaners* are recommended for eliminating odors.
11. *Pee pads*. If necessary due to your living arrangement.

Bringing Home the Puppy

Now it is time to bring your puppy home. There are a couple of things to keep in mind on this day. First, that you are a stranger to him; he has probably never been in a car or away from his mom or littermates. As you can imagine this will be a stressful moment for your puppy, so try to make the ride to your home as stress free as possible.

Before departure, allow your puppy to relieve itself, and during the ride provide a soft comfortable place in a crate or nestled in a humans arms. He may cry or bark during the ride, but that is normal behavior and you must handle it calmly. This will begin to establish that you are there to help. By speaking calmly and evenly, and not speaking harshly, you will show your puppy that you care and are not to be feared. If possible, bring along the entire family and begin the bonding process on the car ride home. Many times the person that brings the puppy to the home is the person that the puppy will begin forming the tightest bond. Drive straight home to keep the drive short. Avoid over handling from family members during the ride home.

If you have to stop for a pee/poop stop, be sure to carry your puppy to an unused area and properly clean up afterward. Your puppy is not yet vaccinated and could have worms or parasites in his feces as well needs to avoid exposure to other dogs.

Ride home checklist

- Cleaning supplies, just in case.
- Soft towel or blanket.
- Collar – if you use a collar be sure it is tight. If you can fit one finger between the collar and your puppy's neck then it is correctly tightened.

- Newspapers, paper towels, and plastic bags.
- Smile, good mood, and cheerful tone of voice.
- Crate (optional).
- Pet odor neutralizer (optional).

First couple of Days and Nights

- Upon arriving home, take him to the predesignated outdoor potty spot.
- Clear the indoor area of other pets and place your puppy down to explore. Do not crowd the puppy and if children are present have them provide the puppy plenty of space. Allow him to come to them on his or her own. Have everyone remain calm and gentle when interacting.
- All puppies act differently. Some take off exploring the house, others just curl up and voyeur the surroundings and might doze off.
- Keep in mind that if your puppy was flown in, or from a shelter that they may have brought stress with them and be extremely tired from the previous day/night. Expect that the following day they will be rested and livelier.
- Separation anxiety is natural and you might hear your puppy whine, squeal, or howl. They might have difficulty sleeping the first few days or weeks. Your puppy has to get used to being away from his sisters, brothers, and mom that he used to snuggle together.
- Move slowly with introducing your other pets to your new puppy. The crate, baby gate, or exercise pen puts a barrier between them and allows both to adjust to one another without direct physical contact.
- After about three or four days, take your puppy to the veterinarian for a complete check-up.

- It is very important to show your puppy that they are wanted and cared for. This is of the utmost importance during the first few days.

"Where does my puppy sleep?"

- The first night will most likely be the most difficult for your puppy, but do not isolate him because he is vocalizing his loneliness. Try not to keep him far from where you are sleeping. He is alone in a strange place, and you want him to feel comfortable and welcomed. For example, do not put him in the garage or basement.
- Options for not isolating your puppy are a dog bed or blanket on the floor near your bed, or in his crate near your bed or just outside the opened bedroom door. For a variety of reasons, it is advised *not* to have your puppy in your bed.
- Even though your puppy is whimpering, do not go to him and pay too much attention every time he is vocalizing distress. This can become a negative behavior used to get you to come to him.

Potty Time

- Take him or her out to relieve themselves every half hour. Soiling accidents are common the first couple of days so clean them thoroughly and use pet deodorizers so that there is no trace. Gradually over the coming days and weeks, you will increase the duration between potty times.
- Always take them to relieve themselves in the designated outdoor potty spot.
- Do not become angry about potty accidents. If you see him going, if possible, pick him up and let him

finish outdoors and afterward praise him while still outdoors.
- Escort your puppy outside and begin praising him for taking care of his potty business.
- To prevent frequent accidents take notice if you need to shorten the time between taking him outside.
- Track your puppies schedule for eating and pees/poops, this can help you eliminate accidents and begins housebreaking. Tracking will help you to learn your puppy's pattern.
- After feeding, always take your puppy outdoors.
- Pick up the water bowl around 8pm each night.
- Always praise your puppy when he or she eliminates waste outdoors and not indoors. This will strengthen your bond and begin building trust.
- Before bedtime, always take your puppy out to relieve themselves. A walk assists them in falling asleep.
- Take your puppy out first thing in the morning.
- Allow him to relieve himself in full. Most puppies will take several small amounts to finish relieving.

Things to Know and Consider

- Always show patience during training and daily interaction.
- Handle your puppy gently.
- Do not strike or yell at your dog.
- Teach good manners from the moment you bring your puppy home.
- Learn about socialization and put it immediately into practice.
- Learn about nutrition and optional diets to implement. Knowing the diet that you will be

providing your new puppy will make your life more relaxed because it eliminates second-guessing.
- Check in with yourself to see if you are being consistent in rule establishment and enforcement. Are you employing the *alpha role* properly?
- Be prepared for your training sessions. Before the session consult your notes to remind yourself of what, where, when you did the last training session.

Puppy Training Prep

You should have already purchased and read a book specifically about your Airedale's personality, care, grooming, and health. Furthermore, if necessary you might have consulted with the breeder and your veterinarian while learning as much as you can about your new puppy. Let's assume that you have done all of these things and you understand the journey that you will be embarking upon, but your puppy is there, frightened in a new home and you have been making him or her feel comfortable and loved beginning with the car ride home. Now you wish to teach your puppy its name and other commands.

Before Training Reminders

- Read your Airedale Terrier breed specific information book and this dog-training book.
- If you have not yet done so, purchase a clicker, leashes, treat pouch, harness, and collar.
- Establish a consistent schedule for feeding, exercise, potty, and playtimes. Should be started as soon as you bring your puppy home.
- Notice if your puppy begins following your around the house. This is a good sign that you are bonding.
- Remember that besides breed traits, all dogs have their own personalities.
- Always be patient, gentle, and kind towards your puppy.
- Begin to observe and get to know your puppy's behaviors including what physical actions they make when they do or do not like something. Observe them during play, exercise, relaxing times, and so forth. Take note of their actions. This helps you to understand your puppy's personality but additionally

assists in identifying possible health issues. This will be an ongoing process throughout the lifetime of your puppy.
- Practice your alpha posture, keeping an even temperament, and clicker timing.
- Read all of the information contained inside the guide before beginning to train. Research and further read anything that needs clarification.
- As a dog owner in training, always keep laughter and light heartedness in mind, because it is of the greatest importance. This is because sometimes training is very difficult on you and your dog. Sometimes your dog will push your patience to the limits. Remember to try and never let your dog know that you are at your limits.
- Keep your humor at the forefront; it will get you through the challenging moments.

Training Landmarks

A. Avoid future problems by early correction of issues. Stop bad behaviors before they escalate.
B. Begin training on the first day that your puppy arrives home. Do not force anything but as the trainer keep all of this in mind.
   - Immediately begin establishing the household rules.
   - Begin house-training.
   - Begin chew-toy training.
   - Begin minimal socialization.
C. Common achievement timelines that should be set up for completion. Footnote on your training calendar and keep track of your puppy's progress. These milestones and your training progress will let you know if you need to solicate help in any of the following.
   - Socialization to humans by 12 weeks.

- Bite/Nipping training successful by 18 weeks.
- *Well socialized* by 5 months of age. At this stage your dog can meet and greet other humans and animals in a calm friendly manner. Your dog handles transportation well and is understanding all basic etiquette for strange encounters. Meeting this goal will set the precedence for your adult dog to have good manners and be trustworthy as an adult. Remain reminded that socialization is a lifetime endeavor.
- *Housetraining* completion ranges from six months to twelve months. Dog size and personality contributes to the training length of time. By four months most puppies often know to wait, but might still have issues. Many puppies are housetrained by six to eight months, or mostly trained by six months with occasional accidents.

Begin Training

Dogs are genetically programmed to hunt, beg, dig, chew, bite, growl, jump, whine, howl, and scavenge. The labels of scavenger or opportunist are appropriate, but they are simply beneficial survival instincts, and dare I say, that we humans share similar. Dogs have a deep, innate hunting instinct that includes digging as a key instrument in their toolbox of survival. Digging is not simply an action that is utilized during the pursuit of prey, but is also an effective survival attribute that assists them in search of roots and other underground foods. All of these behaviors are built into your dog for the benefit and success of living away from their human companions, and your dog should never be considered at fault for expressing them.

Fortunately, these behaviors can be shaped, or curbed to conform to a more desirable and manageable life together. Digging dogs love to dig, and this is a tough one to train out of them, so your best intervention is to allow them a place to dig. Early recognition of your dog's propensity towards a certain behavior will allow you to integrate specific action into your training to target and shape the behavior to your liking, while allowing your dog to express what comes naturally. Negative behaviors, such as biting, chewing, begging, and jumping are conquerable with training and focused behavioral modification, so breathe deep and relax knowing that these challenges have solutions.

Training Outline
- Establishing yourself as the alpha immediately begins with the creation of your puppy's schedule for playtime, food, exercise, and controlling his toys along with providing love and affection. This begins on the first day that you bring your puppy home.
- Simultaneously you will be doing the following, housetraining, establishing your alpha position, and socializing your puppy. After your puppy has been home for a couple of days, you can begin clicker response and training your puppy *name recognition*.
- You should have already read the guide. Begin by gradual socialization to all household members. Be patient, kind, firm, *consistent*, fair, gentle, and have fun.
- Always end training sessions with a win for your puppy while using cheerful upbeat tones when praising.
- Do not forget always to use eye contact when addressing your puppy.

- Remember that training is a lifetime commitment. After your puppy has learned a command, he will need occasional reinforcement to stay sharp and obedient.
- After your puppy knows its name, then you can move onto sit, come, leave it, and other important commands. This training will be concurrently happening while housetraining, chew-toy training, and nipping/biting training is occurring.
- Although you will be training more than one command during your puppy's life, always train only one command per training session. Depending upon how you and your puppy are feeling you can instruct one to three short training sessions per day.
- Remember that when your dog is progressing and learning the commands you can begin phasing out the treats and substituting praise and play as rewards. The end goal is that you have an obedient dog that does not require regular praise for obeying, but every so often be sure that your dog understands that you appreciate his obedience.
- Training a puppy does not mean they are supposed to only obey one master, or alpha, they must learn to obey all commands given to them by the entire family and friend circle. In essence, when you are training, and learning to be a trainer, you also need to teach other family members and friends the correct way to issue these commands.

To begin training, establish your *alpha position* from the moment you bring your new dog or puppy home. Leading as the alpha means that you are always consistent, calm, cool, and collected while consistently enforcing rules and making corrections using a firm but fair attitude. The alpha always acts as though he or she knows that they are in charge. Begin training all new commands indoors. This includes silencing all of your audio-visual devices that act as distractions to dog's sensitive ears.

The best time to begin training your puppy the basics is at around six weeks to eight weeks of age. Once your puppy realizes that you control schedules, toys, mealtimes and all the things he or she cherishes, he or she will respect you as the alpha in the family hierarchy. Remember that all family members and humans are above your dog in ranking, and it should remain that way. Leading as the alpha assists you both in working together towards the goal of understanding the rules of conduct and obedience. Your dog will be at ease when the rules are understood. Remain in control of toys and play time so that your puppy understands that you control all good things. This is important, because if your puppy doesn't have this structure early in life, he or she will grow up thinking that they can do as they wish. No matter how wonderful and easygoing your little puppy seems now, most likely that will change with age.

There exists many different ways to train puppies. Using clicker and rewards based training is an effective and humane way to train dogs. Lying ahead of you will be the task of navigating your dog's unique personality, which will affect your training and relationship. Although, you have no doubt read and watched much about training, spoken with friends and breeders, your dog's personality is why it is imperative to keep an open mind and use your intuition to guide you while training.

Your consent as the owner is the one thing that will allow your dog to become disobedient, out of control, and possibly a danger to your family and the outside world.

Arming yourself with knowledge about dog behaviors, and understanding your own dog's personality will greatly assist you throughout the process of training and companionship alongside your dog. It is your responsibility to guide and train your dog to be a socially adjusted obedient dog so that the two of you have a fruitful relationship.

Below is a list of items that you will need when training your puppy.

Tools of the Trade

- Dog treats
- Dog crate
- Clicker
- Dog collar and harness
- Dog leash 6-foot (2meters) & Long-line 20-30 feet (6-9 meters)
- Treat pouch
- Chew-toys
- Treat dispensing toys
- Books and videos
- **Confident mindset**
- **Sense of humor**

Congratulations on selecting a new puppy and furthermore taking the time to study and learn about the care and training of dogs. Please read forward and pay special attention to the chapters on *socialization and clicker-training* while you begin the adventure of dog training.

Do not forget to download the FREE New Dog Starter Guide that is full of more puppy training information such as the *training mindset,* and *understanding dog communication.*

TRAINING EDUCATION
Unconditional Socialization

What, Where, When, Why

Everyone reads or hears socialization mentioned when reading about dogs and puppies. What is the reason for socialization? When is the best time to socialize my shiny new puppy? These and more, are questions you often hear asked. Does it has to do with getting along well with other dogs and people or is there more to it? Do I let them loose with other dogs and puppies, and just sit back, and watch? Let us begin by looking at how a puppy's social development process is played out from puppy to adulthood.

Socialization is learning and maintaining acceptable behavior in any situation, especially when your dog or puppy does not want too. The goal is learning to handle any normal experience that occurs in life without becoming overly stimulated, fearful, reactive, or aggressive. You want your dog to be able to go with the flow, keep centered, and calm, no matter what the circumstance. Proper socialization of your Airedale Terrier is a crucial part of preparing them for the rest of their life.

Exposure to the many things we take as normal, our little puppies and adult dogs do not. Mechanical noises such as appliances, lawnmowers, car horns, blenders, coffee machines, dishwashers, stereos, televisions, and other similar items are all noises that dogs have to adjust too. Beyond mechanical noises are living creatures, which represents other household pets, neighbor's dogs, and critters in the yard such as gophers, rabbits, squirrels, birds, family members, friends, neighbors, and of course the dreaded stranger.

All of these are new to most eight-week-old puppies arriving at your house. Immediately begin the gradual introduction to these items and living creatures begins from day one. Always be alert to your puppy's reactions and willingness to either dive forward or withdrawal, and never force him or her to interact with things they do not wish too. Proceed at their pace by presenting the interaction and then observing their willingness of participation. When strangers approach your dog do not allow them to automatically reach out and touch, leave a little space and time for your puppy's reaction to be observed, and then you can grant or deny permission based upon your and your puppy's intuition.

Socialization Summary Goals

- Learning to remain calm when the world is buzzing around them.

- Exposure in a safe manner to the environment that will encompass his or her world, including the rules and guidelines that accompany it.

- Learning to respond to signals when they do not want too. For example, In the midst of a tail chasing session with a fellow puppy or the irresistible squirrel.

The first phase of socialization begins as early as 3 weeks and lasts to approximately 12 weeks old, during this time puppies discover that they are dogs and begin to play with their littermates. Survival techniques that they will use throughout their lives, such as biting, barking, chasing, and fighting, begin to be acted out. Concurrently during this time-period, puppies experience big changes socially and physically. Learning submissive postures and taking corrections from their mother, interaction with their littermates begin to teach them about hierarchies. Keeping mother and puppies together for at least 7 weeks tends to increase their ability to get along well with other dogs and learn more about themselves and their actions, such as the force of a bite on their brothers and sisters.

Keep your puppy out of harm's way when he is a little fella, he can easily pick up diseases from sniffing other dog's feces and urine. When you are first exposing your puppy to new people, places, cars, it is good practice to carry him to and from the car. Follow this practice when near any dog clinics, both inside and outside. Keeping your pup protected from contaminated ground surfaces will help keep him healthy. Avoid areas where you suspect other dogs might have eliminated until he has had his vaccines and is a bit older.

Between the ages of 7-12 weeks, a period of rapid learning occurs and they learn what humans are, and whether to accept them as safe. This is a crucial period, and has the *greatest impact* on *all future social behavior*. This is the time we begin teaching puppies the acceptable rules of conduct. Take note that they have a short attention span, and physical limitations. This is the easiest period to get your puppy comfortable with new things, and the chance to thwart later behavioral issues that stem from improper or incomplete socialization. Puppies are not out of harm's way from all diseases at this time, but the risk is relatively low because of primary vaccines, good care, and mother's milk immunity. Behavioral problems are the greatest threat to the owner-dog bond and the number one cause of death to dogs under 3 years of age.

Enrolling your puppy in classes before 3 months of age is an outstanding avenue to improving socialization, training, and strengthening the bond between you and your puppy. You can begin socialization classes as early as 7-8 weeks. The recommendation is to have your puppy receive at least 1 set of vaccines, and a de-worming 7 days prior to starting the first class.

From birth, puppies should be exposed to handling and manipulation of body parts, and exposure to different people, places, situations, well socialized animals, and more. Encourage your puppies exploring, curiosity, and investigation of different environments. Games, toys, and a variety of surfaces such as steps, tile, concrete, tunnels, are all things to expose your puppy too and should continue into adulthood to keep your dog sociable and not shy.

It is important for your puppy to be comfortable playing, sleeping, or exploring alone. Schedule alone play with toys, and solo naps in their crate or another safe area. This teaches them to entertain themselves and not become overly attached, or have separation issues with their owners. Getting them comfortable with their crate is also beneficial for travel and to use as a safe area for your puppy to relax and feel safe.

Having knowledge of your breed and puppy will help in understanding their social predispositions. Some breeds that act as sporting and companion dogs will carry puppy sociability into adulthood. Terriers, guard, herding, and *bully* dogs become less tolerant while others consistently challenge or remain passive.

Two phases of fear imprinting occur in your growing puppy's life. *A fear period is a stage during which your puppy or dog may be more apt to perceive certain stimuli as threatening.* During these two periods, any event your puppy thinks is traumatic can leave a lasting effect, possibly forever. The first period is from 8-11 weeks and the second is between 6-14 months of age. During this period, you will want to keep your puppy clear of any frightening situations, but that is not always easy to determine. A chrome balloon on the floor could possibly scare the "bejeebers" out of your little pup. There is no one size fits all here in knowing what is fearful for your puppy. Becoming familiar with canine body language can help you diagnose your pups fear factor. The second period often reflects the dog becoming more reactive or apprehensive about new things. Larger breeds sometimes have an extended second period.

Keep a few things in mind when seeking play dates for socialization of your puppy. A stellar puppy class will have a safe, mature dog for the puppies to learn boundaries and other behaviors. When making play dates, puppies should be matched by personality and play styles. Games, such as retrieve or drop, help to curb possessive behaviors, as well as to help them learn to give up unsafe or off limits items, so that the item can be taken out of harm's way. Another important lesson during play is for puppies to learn to come back to their human. *Your dog should be willingly dependent upon you and look to you for guidance.*

Teach mature easily stimulated dogs to relax before they are permitted to socialize with others. If you have an adult dog that enjoys flying solo, do not force them into situations. Teach your dogs and puppies less aroused play and encourage passive play. This includes play that does not encompass dominance, mouthing, or biting other puppies. If you have rough play happening between multiple dogs or puppies, then interrupt the rough housing by frequently calling them to you and rewarding their attention. The attention then is turned to you. As a distraction to dissuade mouthing contact, try to interject toys into the play. Elevated play can lead to aggression as they grow, especially breeds that can easily get to full arousal in seconds.

Proper socialization requires patience, kindness, and consistency while teaching. You and your dog should both be having fun during this process. Allow your dog to proceed into new situations at his or her own pace, never force them into a situation that they are not comfortable. If you think that your dog may have a socialization issue, seek professional advice from a qualified behavioral person.

Socializing your puppy, especially before the age of six months, is a very important step in preventing future behavioral problems. Socializing can and should continue throughout the life of your dog. Socializing in a gentle and kind manner prevents aggressive, fearful, and potential behaviors with possible litigious outcomes. A lack of socializing may lead to *fear, aggression, barking,* shyness, *destruction,* territorialism, or *hyperactivity,* and the risk of *wearing Goth make up and the smoking of clove cigarettes*. The earlier you start socializing, the better. However, all puppies and dogs can gradually be brought into new and initially frightening situations, eventually learning to enjoy them. Canines can adapt to various and sometimes extreme situations, they just need your calm, guiding hand.

Expect that the socializing of your dog will be a lifelong endeavor. If your puppy does not engage with other dogs for months or years at a time, you can expect his behavior to be different when he encounters them again. I mean, how would you feel if your sixth grade math teacher, who you haven't seen in 22 years, just walked up and sniffed you?

Here are some methods you can use when exposing your dog to something new, or something he has previously been distrustful contacting:

- Remain calm, upbeat and if he has a leash on, keep it loose.

- Gradually expose him to the new stimulus and if he is wary or fearful never use force. Let him retreat if he needs to.

- Reward your dog using treats; give him a good scratch or an energetic run for being calm and exploring new situations.

Try on a regular basis to expose your dog to the things that you would like him to be capable to cope. His gained familiarity will allow him to calmly deal with such situations in the future. Be careful of the same old-same old. Though dogs love routine, periodically expose your dog to new things. This allows you to assess his need for further socialization. You certainly wouldn't want to go on vacation to the same place every single year, so why would he.

Examples of situations that benefit the social temperament of your Airedale:

- Meeting new kinds of people, including but not limited to, children, crowds, people wearing hats, disabled folks, and people in local services such as postal carriers, fire and police officers, and more. *"Introducing your puppy to a circus clown is saved for another chapter."*

- Meeting new dogs is encouraged. Because of canine diseases, be aware that you should wait at least 4 months before introducing your puppy to dog parks or places where there are groups of adult dogs. You can begin puppy socialization classes at around 7 weeks, just be sure your puppy has a round of vaccines at least a week prior. Slowly expose your dog to other pets, such as cats, horses, birds, llamas, pigs, gerbils, and monitor lizards.

- Your dog's crate is not a jail. Be sure and take the time to teach your puppy to enjoy the comfort and privacy of his own crate. You want your dog's crate to be a place that he or she feels safe. We will be going over instructions on this in the section, Housetraining.

The Importance of Play

When observing dogs in a pack or family, one will notice that dogs and puppies often enjoy playing with one another. During play puppies learn proper play etiquette, such as how hard to bite or mouth, and how rough to play. His mother and littermates provide feedback for him to assist in this learning. Play is instinctual, and as an innate dog behavior, it is something that needs to be satisfied. Humans and dogs both play throughout their lifetime and many studies show that this social interaction is important for the mental and physical health of the individual.

Providing your dog with ample amounts of play through games, such as fetch, tug, or chase helps to satisfy their need for play, and assists in strengthening the bond between dog and owner. When guided in play, your dog will not only acquire the rules of play, but his physical and mental needs will be met during the activity.

One terrific bi-product of play is that it burns off dog's excess energy, and as a result, it helps keep negative behaviors from surfacing. Dogs are naturally full of energy, and they need an outlet to avoid these potential negative behaviors, which includes chewing, digging, and barking. While these behaviors serve them well in the wild, when living with humans they can be a detriment to the harmony and success of the relationship.

Health Insurance for my Dog?
Really? Why?

Because Paying Cash Makes No "Cents" or Does It?
Shocking Statistics! **Discover the Truth!**

healthypaws
PET INSURANCE & FOUNDATION

Protect Your Pet.
Save a Homeless Pet.

TRUSTED BY PET PARENTS
& LOVED BY PETS!

Protect your best friend
and save on vet bills!

☑ Lifetime discounts up to 10%
☑ Unlimited Benefits
☑ #1 Customer-Rated Plan

Quote and Save

Click Here For a Free Quote Now

OR ~ Type Into Your Browser
http://nobrainerdogtrainer.com/insurance-for-dogs/

Separation Anxiety

What is it all about?

Separation anxiety (SA) in dogs is defined as a condition in which a dog exhibits distress and behavioral problems whenever it is separated from its handler. Generally, this behavior will surface within thirty minutes of the separation from the dog's handler.

Separation anxiety can occur not only within puppies, but it can also manifest in adult dogs. With puppies, anxiety related behaviors usually begin when they are first removed from their littermates and mother. The reasons for anxiety behaviors in adult dogs can vary, though they can also be related to the original separation from its family when they were a puppy. Other events that can be responsible for the presence of anxiety in an animal can be related to a traumatic event, such as some type of previous physical injury, mistreatment, and abandonment, all of which can be causes for anxiety related behaviors when separated from its owner.

It must be taken into consideration that some of the normal processes of aging in an animal, such as hearing and sight loss can also contribute to, or exacerbate the potential for higher levels of anxiety. It is important to be able to recognize healthy and abnormal behaviors. By recognizing the signs and symptoms of abnormal behaviors, then you can be prepared to intervene with proactive measures to reduce the negative effects.

Several of the normal behaviors that may occur for those puppies who have recently arrived into a new home can manifest in many ways. Ongoing whining, a constant want for touch or affection, and their need to shadow you wherever you go are some of the most common signs of separation anxiety. Since the puppy is experiencing a variety of new sensations in an unfamiliar environment these behaviors are normal.

The instinct to survive, will motivate a puppy to remain near to their caretaker, thus sticking close to their new provider should be a normal and expected behavior. Often, if a puppy is left alone, he or she will whine, bark, or even howl to express their discomfort from being alone. Your dog's individual personality will dictate how long these behaviors last during your absence. It is common that your dog will find something to pacify itself in this alone time, such as gnawing upon one of his chewy toys. It is usual for these behaviors to cease after a short time, and should not be an ongoing, day and night occurrence that last regularly over thirty minutes. Yes, these sounds can be distressing to listen to, but remember that they are normal expressions while they learn to adapt to their new environment. Do not be alarmed because this is just a phase in their development, and it will soon pass.

Allowing your new puppy to remain alone for periods of time, is a necessary component of his socialization training which allows him to experience time alone and gradual exposure to mechanical noises, other humans, animals, and the exciting world of his new environment. As said prior, it is important to keep in mind that sometimes the upsetting behaviors he displays are normal but they will subside over time. Positive training in combination with consistent socialization will empower your puppy to overcome these anxieties and gain the self-confidence to develop into a well-adjusted adult dog. Training sessions work as an important component for building self-confidence and a puppy's character, but in itself is not a cure for separation anxiety.

Deeper Separation Anxiety

Identifying a puppy or adult dog that is experiencing a deeper, chronic anxiety can be detected by an awareness that his separation behaviors are heightened and frequently displayed. Clinically, this would be diagnosed by a veterinarian as a chronic, pathological form of separation anxiety, and may need psychological or medical intervention. For example, extended durations of whining, barking, or crying lasting thirty minutes to an hour or more is an indication of a greater problem. In extreme cases, this heightened behavior might be intermixed with a more frantic barking, and perhaps howling or whining that may continue until your puppy becomes completely exhausted from his expressions of stress.

Other signs of anxiety can appear in an inability to remain calm or still, acting out by pacing rapidly, spinning in place, or jumping up and down sometimes in a hysterical and frantic manner. While being contained in his crate or gated area, he might tear excessively at the interior, his blankets, flooring, toys, or anything else he can get his little razor teeth, or tiny paws into. This behavior should be recognized not as a regular chewing behavior that well-adjusted dogs' display, but instead intentional destructive behavior, physically acting out his anxiety and deep-rooted distress.

Signs of *stress* also can manifest in the form of drooling, continuous panting, and frequent yawning. Loss of bladder and bowel control can lead to frequent accidents, and diarrhea and loose stools are common when an animal is stressed. Obsessive-compulsive behaviors such as excessive gnawing, licking or chewing upon his own body, including the feet need to be treated by a veterinarian.

If your dog is displaying signs of depression, anxiety, or excessive excitement each time you prepare to leave, or if his greetings are hysterical and unrestrained, and he is following you from room to room, these are indicators of separation anxiety, and need immediate attention.

If you have determined that your puppy is suffering from Separation Anxiety by his signs and symptoms, then you have to begin the important journey of teaching your puppy that not everything is bad nor has a potential for lasting trauma or discomfort. Instead, teach him that his new environment and the world is a nurturing place, not something to be feared, and that if you are not around, his world will not end. Treating your puppy's issues will take some time and patience and perhaps some assistance from professionals who are trained in these animal behaviors.

Preventing Separation Anxiety from developing is the best plan to undertake, first beginning in puppyhood, and then following up with your adult dog who perhaps exhibits the symptoms. Following these simple steps below should keep your puppy or full-grown dog from developing or displaying any severe behaviors and reduce the symptoms of separation anxiety.

Prevention of Separation Anxiety

- Your new pup is the cutest fur-ball of joy that you have ever seen, *right*. Heck, you picked him out of the litter and brought him home to become a member of your family. Although the desire to hold, coddle, cuddle, and fondle our pets whenever possible, may be a deep part of our human nature, it is during these times of innate urges to display a little restraint.

As difficult as I know it can be, refrain from carrying him around with you wherever you go and limit your compulsion to shower him with constant, syrupy affection. These actions, though pleasing to the both of you, can serve as the catalyst for the onset of separation anxiety. These actions create a dependency for that loving warmth that you lavish on him. If not nipped in the bud early on, this will be more difficult to curb in the future.

- Whether awake or asleep, give your little pup some space of his own. A little distance and autonomy goes a long way to help create healthy independence. Remember as you are doing this, it is neither cruel nor neglect, but in actuality this distance constitutes an essential element of the proactive measures that will help him feel secure when he is on his own.

What you want to avoid is creating a puppy that never wants to leave your side, and is in constant fear of being away from the safety, comfort and attention that you may continually bestow upon him. Although well intended, the attention that you may continually shower on him will result in having a "shadow" dog, which will neither benefit you, nor will it be healthy for him. Give him some space throughout your days together, and resist the craving to keep him with you everywhere you go.

- Begin leaving your puppy alone from the first day that you bring him home. Whether contained in his crate or restricted to his gated area, I advise that keep you keep him out of eyesight. Start the periods of separation with short durations of about 2-4 minutes each. As he begins to cope with this initial interval without freaking out and becoming agitated, then gradually, increase the extent of time that he is left alone. Leaving your pup alone should be done at least two or three times per day. During this time, it is essential to *ignore* any of his whimpering, whining, or any other form of agitation he may express. Do not confuse this exercise with neglect.

- *How to act when leaving your puppy alone.* Don't make a big deal of it when you are leaving, especially by showing exaggerated or disproportionate emotions that may in fact display your own *human separation anxiety.* This is dangerously contagious to our canine friends. Before you depart, simply make sure he is confined in an area that is of a comfortable temperature, that he has plenty of chew-toys, and fresh water. Oh! In addition, please don't forget to let the little guy relieve himself before you take off.

  In the moment of your departure, use a positive tone of voice and a brief expression of farewell, using a simple phrase, such as "Goodbye, be back soon," will suffice. Stay clear of sappy, long and drawn out emotional partings. If you make a dramatic sendoff, this may become the creation of fear and concern, setting into motion a situation that may promote an elevation in the level of anxiety he will experience as you leave, thus resulting in all of the negative behaviors associated with SA.

- *Act similar upon returning.* Upon returning home, do not immediately make eye contact with your pup, or run to him as though it has been days since you have seen each other. If you have been gone for over an hour, then it is fine to go pick him up and say hello, immediately followed by a relief break. When he is finished with his business, place him back into his puppy area and return to your business. If you have only been away for a few minutes, a casual hello or

quick pet will suffice, and it is not necessary to immediately make eye contact with him, or even acknowledge his existence.
- As I have covered in prior material, as part of supporting good puppy health and maintaining your alpha dominance, it is important to set a consistent schedule for feeding, playing, training, and relieving times by creating a routine of the activities for daily living.
- *Human advice.* Control your temper; he cannot help his crying out for attention. If your puppy is getting upset and simply driving you crazy with his whimpering, crying, barking, or howling, remember to keep your alpha composure by being even-tempered, firm, fair, and consistent in your actions. Keep in mind that *you* are in charge and it is *you* that dictates the rules and schedules, *not your darling, adorable little sidekick.*

Troubleshooting Separation Anxiety

If you have a puppy or an adult dog that is displaying what appears to be clinical symptoms of moderate to severe separation anxiety, it is likely that professional interventions need to be sought out, followed by more advanced and focused training methods. Even though S.A. occurs in a very small percentage of domestic dogs, a dog with separation anxiety will nonetheless make life difficult for you and your family. If left untreated, this can lead to health complications and ongoing behavioral problems.

If your puppy or adult dog has a range of negative behaviors ranging from excessive destruction of property, fearfulness, barking, whimpering, whining, or anxiousness, then below are some techniques that can be used to relieve some of the symptoms. If your dog is suffering from some these behaviors, it is possible that with your proactive measures and concerted efforts your dog will be capable of displaying calmer mannerisms and an improved mental health. Reducing the effects SA is having upon your puppy will also greatly improve your mental health status.

Minor symptoms of nervousness can be handled with some simple dog training techniques.

- Remove *boredom* from your puppy's life. Supply plenty of chew-toys, at least 30- minutes of daily vigorous exercise (age appropriate), one to two daily training sessions of obedience commands, and socialization sessions.
- Exercise in the form of a brisk walk or short game of fetch before your planned absence can burn away any surplus energy reserves that if not expended can serve to trigger further anxiousness during your absence.
- While you are gone, it can be soothing to leave a low volume radio or television on to distract or comfort him. *Prior to doing this*, test it out to see if it is actually soothing rather than agitating your puppy.
- Occupy alone time with stuffed chew-toys. These toys can be stuffed in such a way that make it a time consuming project for him to extract the food, thus keeping him distracted for long periods of time. The nice thing about these chew toys is that it is impossible to bark, whine, or cry while chewing them.

Moderate symptoms will appear as more severe than the features of minor nervousness, and needs to be tackled with more intensive behavioral modification techniques that will require daily practice through focused dog training that can take weeks or months to solve the issue.

- First, increase the daily exercise routine keeping within the recommended limits of your puppy's breed. Take care to make sure your little pup does not overheat, and if he is an extra-large breed be careful that he is not jumping or doing anything that may injure his growing bones.
Begin multiple daily rigorous exercise regimens that utilize games, brisk walks, and if possible, fit in 2-3 outings of fetch games. If your dog refuses to play fetch, then substitute some other type of play or exercise that will increase his heart rate and use up some of his energy reserves. Try for a minimum of two 30-minute activity based periods per day.
- Two daily short 10-minute training sessions of the basic commands, followed by teaching down-stay or sit-stay is advised. The commands of sit-stay and down-stay are great in creating confidence in your dog so that he can be left alone by teaching him to accept distance between the two of you in different places, and at different times.
- Another great option is that when your puppy is old enough, and had at least his first round of shots, is to enroll him into a puppy kindergarten class. This will increase his socialization skills, and build confidence under the guidance of a trained professional. These classes also instruct humans on how to train and interact with their puppies.
- If you have a dog that we refer to as a "Shadow dog," which means a dog that refuses to leave your side, then it is essential that you work on gradually increasing the space between the two of you. This is easy to do by using his crate or gated area as his isolation areas, and progressively increasing the duration that you are separated. Beginning with short

durations of time apart or when you notice a pause in his fretting is the time you should free him from his confines. When you free him from his confines, be sure not to make a big deal about it, act as if it is just a normal daily routine. Take special care and make appropriate adjustments if your dog is still displaying destructive behaviors or becoming extremely agitated in his isolation areas, especially in his crate. If this is the case, do not use his crate for this particular training. We want our puppies to love their crates and find them a safe haven.

Desensitizing your puppy to your absence is another way to help him through the miseries of his separation anxiety. Sometimes the simplest action, such as grabbing your jacket, bag or the sounds of keys clanging can be a stimulus for your puppy begin to feel anxious in anticipation of your absence.

- To begin to desensitize your puppy to your departures, start by acting out the preparations to leave, but not actually leaving the house. Go through the motions, such as grabbing your house keys, or briefcase, but instead of leaving, just walk around the house for a couple of minutes carrying your things. After doing that, put your things away. Practice this three to five times a day until your dog ceases showing signs of agitation or nervousness during your *faux departure* preparations. The success of this training varies in duration from dog to dog. Depending upon your dog and his predisposition, this training could take a day, a couple of days, a week, or even longer.
- The next step is to repeat the step above, but now leave the premises. Begin by leaving for only a few

seconds and then returning indoors. During this training, gradually increase the time that you wait outside of your house before returning inside. The key here is never to make a big deal of leaving or coming home, just act as if it is an event not worthy of attention or emotion. Simply grab your things and leave. Continue this training until your dog becomes less and less disturbed by this whole affair of you coming and going.
- Upon returning home after a lengthy leave, walk inside and immediately tend to your normal life, ignoring your dog for at least five to ten minutes. After this duration, or when you are ready to show attention and affection, then go to your dog and give him the love he deserves.

How to lessen your dog's symptoms when you are going to leave

1. Take your pup for a quick fast-paced walk or vigorous exercise session.
2. Turn on the radio or television to lessen the loneliness. If this has proved to be soothing and not agitating.
3. Leave plenty of toys to keep him busy.
4. When you leave, leave quickly without emotional outpourings towards your dog.

Extra Helpings for Separation Anxiety Training

1. Hire a pet sitter or dog walker to visit at least once during the day.
2. Ask your neighbors how your dog is acting while you are away.
3. Once or twice a week, drop your dog at a doggie day-care facility.

4. If the dog training tips within this guide do not seem to work for you, solicit outside help from a professional trainer and speak with your veterinarian.
5. As a last resort, after trying all of the suggestions above, there are medications available to help calm your dog. I recommend that this is a temporary solution, as a part of a holistic therapy, *while you continue* to shape and change your dog's behavior using the methods and techniques described. If choose to use medication, research for the safest natural product on the market, or rely on the advice of your dog's vet.
6. Avoid leaving your dog crated for long periods.
7. Avoid punishments for SA related accidents or incidents. Remember that because of the deep-seated nature of his problem, a dog with SA is not in control of himself. For example, as demonstrated by soiling issues related to his anxieties.

The goal and final outcome of this training is to have a healthy, happy, well-adjusted dog that can handle any situation that comes his way. As previously mentioned, prevention of Separation Anxiety can afford you the peace of mind knowing that you will not have to go through this rigorous training, as well as never having to deal with the aggravation of incessant whimpering, barking, gnawing, tearing, and other doggie anxiety actions that will negatively affect you, your family, visiting friends and your neighbors. Some statistics indicate that only about 10-15% of the population of domestic dogs become afflicted with some degree of separation anxiety.

Handling Training

Teaching your Aire to be still, calm, and patient while he is being handled is a very important step in your relationship. When you master this one, it will make life easier for both of you when at home, and either at the groomer or the vet. It also helps when there is unwanted or accidental touching and especially when dealing with small children who love to handle dogs in all sorts of unusual and not so regular ways. This one will take patience and a few tricks to get it started. Remember, it is important to begin handling your new puppy immediately after you find each other and are living together.

Understand that muzzles are not bad and do not hurt dogs. They can be an effective device and a great safety feature when your dog is learning to be handled. Easy cheese or peanut butter spread on the floor or on the refrigerator door should keep your puppy in place while he learns to be handled. If your puppy does not like to be handled, he can slowly learn to accept it.

You must practice this with your puppy for at least one to three minutes each day so that he becomes comfortable with being touched. All dogs are unique and therefore some will accept this easier and quicker than others will. Handling training will be a life-long process.

With all of the following exercises, follow these steps:

- Begin with short, non-intrusive gentle touching. *If your puppy is calm* and he is not trying to squirm away, use a word such as "good," "nice," or "yes," and give your pup a treat.

- If your puppy squirms, keep touching him but do not fight his movements, keeping your hands lightly on him while moving your hand with his squirms. When he settles, treat him and remove your hands.

- Work from one second to ten seconds where applicable, gradually working your way up to touching for longer durations, such as 2,4,6,8 to 10 seconds.

- Do not go forward to another step until your puppy adapts to, and enjoys the current step.

- *Do not* work these exercises more than a couple of minutes at a time. Overstimulation can cause your puppy stress. Continue slowly at your puppy's comfortable speed.

Handling the Body

Paws in the clause

It is a fact that most puppies do not like to have their paws touched. Proceed slowly with this exercise. The eventual goal is for your puppy to adore his paws being fondled. In the following exercises, any time your puppy does not squirm and try to get away, *click and treat* your pup. If he does squirm, stay with him using gentle contact, when your pup ceases wiggling, then *click and treat*, and release when he calms down. Each one of these steps will take a few days to complete and will require at least a dozen repetitions. Make sure you successfully complete each step and your puppy is at least tolerant of the contact before you go on to the next one.

- *Do each step with all four paws, and remember to pause a minute between paws, allowing your pup to regain his composure.*

- Pick up your puppy's paw and immediately click and treat. Repeat this five times and then continue forward by adding an additional one second each time you pick up his paw until ten seconds is reached.

- Hold the paw for ten-twelve seconds with no struggling from your dog. Begin with two seconds then in different sessions work your way to twelve.

- Hold the paw and move it around.

- Massage the paw.

- Pretend to trim the nails.

Side Note: Do not trim your dog's nails unless you are positively sure you know what you are doing. It is not easy and it can cause extreme pain to your dog if you are not properly trained.

The Collar

Find a quiet, low distraction place to practice, grab treats, and put your puppy's collar on him.

- While gently restrained, touch your dog's collar underneath his chin, and then release him right away simultaneously clicking and treating him. Do this about ten times or until your puppy seems comfortable and relaxed with it.

- Grab and hold the collar where it is under his chin and hold it for about 2 seconds, C/T, and repeat. Increase the amount of time until you have achieved about ten seconds of holding and your puppy remains calm. Click and treat after each elapsed amount of time. Work your way up 2,4,6,8 to 10 seconds of holding. This may take several days and sessions.

- Hold the collar under his chin and now give it a little tug. If he accepts this and does not resist, click and treat, and repeat. If he squirms, keep a gentle hold on the collar until he calms down, and then C/T and release him. Repeat this step until he is content with it.

Now, switch to the top of the collar and repeat the whole progression again. Remember slowly increase the time held and the intensity of the tug using a slow pace.

You can pull or tug, but *do not jerk* your puppy's neck or head because this could cause injury and interfere with your outcome objectives of the training exercise. You can practice touching the collar while you are treating during training other tricks. Gently hold the bottom or top of the collar when you are giving your dog a treat reward for successfully completing a commanded behavior.

From the mouth of dog's

- Gently touch your puppy's mouth, *click and treat*, and repeat ten times.

- Touch the side of your puppy's mouth and lift a lip to expose a tooth, *click and treat*, then release only after he stops resisting.

- Gently and slowly, lift the lip to expose more and more teeth on both sides of the mouth, and then open the mouth. Then release when he does not resist, *click and treat*. Be cautious with this one.

- Touch a tooth with a toothbrush, then work up to brushing your puppy's teeth for one to ten-seconds, and then later increase the time. Brushing your puppy's teeth is something you will be doing a few times weekly for the lifetime of your dog.

Do you ear what I ear?

- Reach around the side of your puppy's head, and then briefly and gently touch his ear. Click and treat, repeat ten times.

- When your puppy is comfortable with this, continue and practice holding the ear for one-second. If he is calm, click and treat. If he squirms, stay with him until he is calm. When your puppy calms down, click and treat, then release the ear. Do this until ten seconds is completed with no wiggling.

- Maneuver your pup's ear and pretend that you are cleaning it. Do this gently and slowly so that your puppy learns to enjoy it. It will take a few days of practice until your puppy is calm enough for the real ear cleaning. If your puppy is already sensitive about his ears being touched, it will take longer. See ear cleaning in the Basic Care section.

Proceed slowly at your puppy's comfortable pace. There is no rush, only the end goal of your pup enjoying being handled by you in all sorts of ways that are beneficial to him.

A tell of the tail

Many puppies are sensitive about having their tails handled, and rightly so. Think about if someone grabs you by the arm and you are not fully ready. That is similar to the reaction a puppy feels when grabbed, especially when their tails are handled.

- Start by briefly touching his tail. When moving to touch your puppy's tail move slowly and let your hand be seen moving towards his tail. This keeps your puppy from being startled. Repeat this ten times with clicking and treating, until you notice your puppy is comfortable with his tail being touched.

- Increase the duration of time you hold his tail until you achieve the ten-second mark.

- Tenderly and cautiously, pull the tail up, brush the tail, and then tenderly pull on it until your dog allows you to do this without reacting by jerking, wiggling, or whimpering.

Children, 'nuff said

You must prepare your poor puppy to deal with the strange, unwelcome touching that is often exacted on them by children. Alternatively, you could just put a sign around his neck that says; "You must be at least 16 to touch this puppy." However, it is very likely that your puppy will encounter children that are touchy, grabby, or pokey.

- Prepare your puppy for the strange touches that children may perpetrate. Prepare him by practicing while clicking and treating him for accepting these odd bits of contact such as ear tugs, tail tugs, and perhaps a little harder than usual head pats, kisses, and hugs. Keep in mind, as previously mentioned, puppies and kids are not a natural pairing, *but cheese and wine are*. Even a puppy that is *good with kids* can be pushed to a breaking point and then things can get ugly.

Always supervise children around your dog. ALWAYS! – It is a dog ownership law.

Can you give me a lift?

An emergency may arise that requires you to pick up your dog. As you do these maneuvers, move and proceed slowly and cautiously. First, briefly put your arms around your dog and then give him a click and treat if he stays still.

Increase the time duration with successive repetitions. Your dog should be comfortable for ten to fifteen seconds with your arms around him. Next, slowly proceed lifting your dog off the ground and back down, then click and treat when he does not wriggle. Increase the time and the distance you that you lift him from the ground and then move your dog from one place to another. Calculate the time it might take to lift and carry your dog from the house and place him into your vehicle. This is a good time goal to set for carrying your dog.

Eventually, by lifting your dog up and placing him on a table, you will be able to prepare your dog for trips to the groomer, open spaces, or the vet. If you own an extra-large dog, or dog that is too heavy for you to lift, solicit help for this training from family or a friend. *Gigantor* may take two to lift safely and properly, or use one of the methods below.

Once up on the table you can practice handling in ways a groomer or veterinarian might handle your dog. This is good preparation for a day at the dog spa or veterinary procedures.

Ways to lift a dog

To lift a large dog properly, always start by approaching the dog from the side. Place one of your hands upon the dog's rear end with the tail in the down position, unless it is a curly tailed spitz type dog that will not enjoy having its tail forced down. This protects the dog's tail from being forced painfully upwards should your arm slip. You should be holding your dog directly underneath the dog's rear hips. Your other hand should be in the front of the dog around his front legs with your arm across his chest. Now your arms should be on your dog's chest and butt area.

Then gently press your arms together as in a cradling position and lift using your legs. The human's body position should be that of having bent legs and crouching down so that the power in the legs is used to lift you and your dog upright. To prevent injury to yourself, keep your back as straight as possible.

Small dogs are simpler to lift and require much less effort, but still take great care not to inadvertently injure them. Place your hand in between the back and front legs underneath the dog's underbelly. Supporting the rear with your forearm and placing a hand on the dogs chest is a good idea for extra safety in case your dog squirms when being lifted.

For extra-large or dogs that are too heavy for you to lift, purchase and utilize a ramp so that your dog can walk itself into your vehicle. This saves you and your dog from possible or inevitable injury. It is always best to use caution instead of risking a painful, costly, or permanent injury. Of course, you can also teach your dog to jump into the vehicle. Later when your dog becomes aged, you can then utilize the ramp.

Some large dogs can be taught to put their front paws up onto the vehicle floorboard or tailgate, thus allowing you to help push them from their buttocks and assist them jumping in your vehicle.

Never grab, pull, or lift a dog by its fore or rear legs. This can cause serious pain and injury to a dog.

The brush off

- Get your puppy's brush and lightly touch him with it all over his body. If he remains unmoving, give him a click and treat, then repeat. Repeat this until you can brush his whole body and he does not move.

Your puppy will become comfortable with all varieties of touching and handling if you work slowly, patiently, and with plenty of good treats. Handling training is a very important step in your dog's socialization to make him comfortable with being handled.

Clicker Training

Why and How Clicker Training Works

The important reason I put this information together is that it is essential to understand why timing and consistency is important, and why clicker training works. If any of this is confusing, do not worry, because I walk you through the training process, step-by-step.

Clicker training started over seventy years ago and has become a tried and true method for training dogs and other animals. The outcome of using a clicker is an example of conditioned reinforcement. Rewarding the animal in combination with clicker use has proven highly effective as a positive reinforcement training method. It is a humane and effective way of training dogs without instilling fear for non-compliance. I know that my mother wished she would have known about clicker training when my brother and I were growing up. I am sure she would have put the clicker into action so my brother would place his dirty clothes inside the bin, rather than on the floor.

In the 1950s, Keller Breland, a pioneer in animal training, used a clicker while training many different species of animals, including marine mammals. He met great success using this method of training on these animals. His system developed for clicker training marine mammals is still in use today. Keller also trained dogs using the clicker. Because of its effectiveness, it was brought into use by others in the dog training community. Gradually, clicker training for dogs gained more and more popularity and by the early 1980's its use became widespread. The success of the clicker spans 7 decades and now is a widely accepted standard for dog training.

A trainer will use the clicker to mark desired actions as they occur. At the exact instant, the animal performs the desired action, the trainer clicks and promptly delivers a food reward or other reinforcements. One key to clicker training is the trainer's timing, as *timing is crucial*. For example, clicking and rewarding slightly too early or too late will reinforce the action that is occurring at that very instant rather than the action you were targeting the reward for. The saying goes, "you get what you click for."

Clicker trainers often use the process of *shaping*. Shaping is the process of gradual transformation of a specific action into the desired action by rewarding each successive progression towards the desired action. This is done by gradually molding or training the dog to perform a specific response by first, reinforcing the small, successive responses that are similar to the desired response, instead of waiting for the perfect completion to occur. The trainer looks for small progressions that are heading in the direction towards the total completion of the desired action and then clicks and treats. It is important to recognize and reward those tiny steps made in the target direction. During training, the objective is to create opportunities for your dog to earn frequent rewards. In the beginning, it is acceptable to increase the frequency of a C/T to every 3-4 seconds, or less. By gauging the dog's abilities and improvements, the trainer can gradually increase the length of time between C/T. It is necessary to assess the dog's progress from moment to moment, adjusting C/T to achieve the desired actionable outcome.

During training, and in conjunction with clicker use, the introduction of a cue word or hand signal can be applied. Eventually, the clicker can be phased out in favor of a cue or cues that have been reinforced during the training sessions. As a result, your dog will immediately respond by reacting, obeying, and performing actions to your hand gestures or verbal commands. Watching this unfold is a highly satisfying process, which empowers your friend to be the best he can, and while you have fulfilled your role as *alpha* and pack leader.

Why is clicking effective over using a word cue first?

The clicking sound is a unique sound that is not found in nature, and it is more precise than a verbal command. Verbal commands can be confusing because the human voice has many tonal variations, whereas the clicker consistently makes a sound that your dog will not confuse with any other noise. It is also effective because it is directed at him and followed by good things. Therefore, your dog completely understands which action is desired and your dog will quickly understand that the click is followed by a reward.

The clicker sound is produced in a quick and accurate way that is in response to the slightest actions that your dog makes. This clarity of function of this tool increases the bond between you and your dog, as a result making your dog more interested in the training sessions, and ultimately your relationship more engaging and entertaining. Dare I say fun? On that note, do not forget to always have fun and add variety to your training sessions.

Variety is the spice of life, mix up those treats, rewards, and commands.

Clicker training works this way

At the *exact* instant the action occurs, the trainer clicks. If a dog begins to *sit*, the trainer recognizes that, and *at the exact moment the dog's buttocks hits the ground the trainer clicks and offers the dog a reward*. Usually the reward is a small kernel sized food treat, but a reward can be a toy, play, or affection. Whatever the dog enjoys is a reward worth giving.

In as soon as 2-3 clicks have been issued a dog will associate the sound of the click with something it enjoys. Once the association is made, it will repeat the action it did when hearing the click. Click = Reward. When this goes off in the dog's head, repeating the action makes sense.

The three steps are as follows:

1. *Get the action* you request

2. *Mark the action* with your clicker

3. *Reinforce the action* with a reward

How do you ask for actions when clicker training your dog?

During clicker training before adding a cue command such as "stay," you wait until your dog completely understands the action. A cue is the name of the action or it can be a hand signal that you are using when you ask your dog to perform a specific action. Your dog should know the action *stay* from the click and reward before you verbally name it. *He or she has connected being still to receiving a click and reward.*

When training you do not want to add the *cue* until your dog has been clicked 5-10 times for the action, and is accurately responding in a manner that clearly shows he understands which action earns the click and reward. This is called introducing the cue.

Teaching your dog the name of the cue or action requires saying or signaling before your dog repeats the action. After several repetitions, begin to click and reward when your dog performs the action, be sure the cue is given before the reward. Your dog will learn to listen and watch for the cue, knowing that if he does the action a reward will follow.

Clicker Training Help

If your dog is not obeying the cue, answer the following questions and then revise your training process so that your dog knows the meaning of the clicker sound cue during all situations. Importantly, be sure that your dog is and feels rewarded for doing the correct action.

Trainers never assume the dog is intentionally disobeying without asking the questions below.

1. Does your dog understand the meaning of the cue?

2. Does your dog understand the meaning of the cue in the situation first taught, but *not* in the different situations that you gave the cue?

3. Is the *reward* for doing the action you want, satisfying your dog's needs? Is the treat or toy worth the effort?

Once you have answered these questions, change your training process to be certain that your dog understands the clicker/cue in all situations, including high distraction situations such as at a busy park. Then be sure your dog is adequately rewarded and that it is clear your dog feels that he or she has been properly rewarded. This will help put you two back on the path of mutual understanding during your training sessions.

When starting to train a new command ease into it by practicing a couple of repetitions of a command that your dog already knows. This establishes a training session and gains your dog's attention. Try to end all training sessions with success, either by ending with a previously learned command or a successful action of the current command being taught. Ending training sessions on high notes keeps your dog's mind positive. Play or free time after each training session further enforces that training is something they should look forward too.

Clicker Q&A

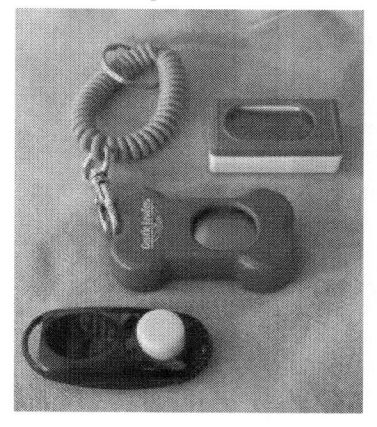

What the heck is that clicking noise? Well, it's a clicker, thus the name. If you are a product of a Catholic school, you might be very familiar with this device. You probably have nightmares of large, penguin like women clicking their way through your young life. Yes, it was annoying and at times, terrifying, however, when it comes to training your dog, it will be helpful and fun.

A clicker is a small device that makes a sound that is easily distinguished and not common as a sound in nature, or one that humans normally produce. This unique sound keeps the dog that is being trained from becoming confused by accidently hearing a word used in conversation or another environmental noise. You click at the exact time when your dog does the correct action then immediately follow the click with a treat or reward.

The clicker is used to inform your dog that he did the right thing and that a treat is coming. When your dog does the right thing after you command, like drop your Chanel purse that is dangling from his mouth, you click and reward him with a nice treat. Using the clicker system allows you to set your puppy up to succeed while you ignore or make efforts to prevent bad behavior. It is a very positive, humane system, and punishment is *not* part of the process.

Here are some questions often asked about the clicker training:

- "Do you need to have the clicker on your person at all times?" *No.* The clicker is a teaching device. Once your dog understands what you want your dog to do, you can then utilize a verbal or hand cue, and if inclined verbal praise or affection.

- "Can rewards be other things besides treats?" *Sure.* Actually, you should mix it up. Use the clicker and a treat when you first start teaching. When your puppy has learned the behavior you want, then switch to other rewards, such as, petting, play, toys, or lottery tickets. Remember always to ask for the wanted target behavior, such as, *sit*, *stay*, or *come*, before you reward your dog. These verbal reinforcements can augment the clicker training and reward giving.

- "With all these treats, isn't my dog going to get fat?" *No.* If you figure treats into your dog's daily intake and subtract from meals accordingly, your dog will be fine. The treats should be as small as a corn kernel, just a taste. Use food from his regular meals when you are training indoors, but when outdoors, use fresh treats like meat or cheese. There are many distractions outside and a tasty fresh treat will help keep your puppy's attention. Dog's finally honed senses will smell even the smallest of treat, and this keeps them attentive. -"What do I do if my dog doesn't act out the command?" *Simpl*e, if your dog disobeys you, it is because he has not been properly trained yet. Do not C/T (Click and Treat), or verbally praise for any wrong actions, ignore the wrong action. Continue training because your dog has not yet learned the command and action you are teaching him to perform. He, after all, is just a dog. If he is disobeying, he has been improperly or incompletely trained, maybe the treats are not tasty enough. Try simplifying the task and attempt to make the reward equal to, or better than what is distracting your dog. Eventually your dog will understand what action should be performed when the command word is spoken.

HELPFUL HINT

- *Conceal the treat! Do NOT* show your dog the treat before pressing the clicker and making the clicking sound. If you do this, he will be responding to the treat and not the click and this will *undermine* your training strategy.

Training Pointers

Knowing what you want to train your dog to do is as important as training your dog. You can begin training almost immediately, at around six weeks of age. A puppy is a blank slate and does not know any rules, therefore it is a wise idea to make a list and have an understanding of what you would like your puppy to do. What are the household rules and proper dog etiquette? As he grows, the same principle applies and you may adjust training from the basics to more specialized behaviors, such as making your dog a good travel, hiking, agility, hunting, or simply a companion dog. Know what conditions and circumstances you plan to expose your dog or puppy to outside of the household and strategize to be prepared for those encounters by slowly introducing your dog to those situations.

Establish yourself as the pack leader from the time you first bring your new dog or puppy home. Being the *alpha* assists in the training process, and your dog's relationship with you and your family. Life is much easier for your dog if you are in charge, leading, and providing for his needs.

Leading as the alpha assists in the act of working together with your dog towards the goal of understanding the rules of conduct and obedience. Your dog will be at ease when the rules are understood. Training should be an enjoyable bonding time between you and your dog. Remember that there is no set time limit defining when your dog should learn, understand, and then obey commands. Use short training sessions and be aware that if either of you are tired, it is recommended that you stop and try again later. If something does not seem quite right with your dog, in any way, have him checked out by a veterinarian.

Timing is crucial when rewarding for good behaviors and making corrections for bad. *Patience and Consistency* are your allies in the training game. An easy way to avoid the onset of many different behavioral problems is to give your dogs or puppies ample daily exercise to keep them fit and healthy, and destructive behavioral problems at bay. Always provide consistent structure, firm but fair authority, rule enforcement, and importantly, love and affection. By maintaining these things, you will help to create a loyal companion and friend. Reward good behaviors, not for simply being cute, sweet, loveable, and huggable. If you wish to reward your dog, always reward after you issue a command and your dog obeys appropriately.

Only train one command per session. Puppies only have the attention span to go about 10 minutes per session, but never exceed 15 minutes. Training a command once per day is enough for your dog to begin to learn and retain, but whenever the opportunity presents itself you should reinforce the training sessions throughout the day. For example, opening a door or putting down a food bowl first command sit, down or stay and be sure not to reward your dog unless your dog obeys. The most important thing to remember is to remain relaxed, keep it fun, and enjoy this time of bonding and training your dog or puppy.

All dogs have their own personalities and therefore respond to training differently. No matter the breed that comes with its own characteristics, you need to account for individual personality and adjust accordingly. If needed, do not hesitate to solicit professional help and advice.

We all love treats, and so does your dog. Giving your dog a treat is the best way to reinforce good behavior, to help change his behavior or just to make your dog do that insanely funny dance- like-thing he does. Make the treats small enough for him to get a taste, but not a meal, kernel sized. Remember, you do not want him filling up on treats as it might spoil his dinner and interfere with his attention span.

- Keep a container of treats handy with you at all times. You do not want to miss a chance to reward a good behavior or reinforce a changed behavior. Always carry treats when you go on a walk. Remember what treats your dog likes most and save those for super special times. In addition, what you consider a treat and what your dog considers a treat are two vastly different worlds. A single malt scotch or chicken wings might be a treat in your mind, but dried liver bits or beef jerky in your dogs.

- Ask for something before you give the treat. Tell your dog to sit, stay, or lie down, print two copies of your resume, anything, before you reward your dog with treats, petting, or play. By asking for good behavior, before you give your dog a reward, you demonstrate you are in charge, in an easy fun manner. There is a common misconception that dogs are selfless and wanting to behave only to please out of respect for you. This is horse pucky. This line of thinking is incorrect and detrimental to your success with the training. You have to make sure that your dog knows exactly why he should be listening to you. You are the alpha, the keeper of the treats, the provider of the scratching and the purveyor of toys. Keep this balance of power and the results will be your reward.

- Be positive. Think about what you want your dog to do, instead of what you don't want him to do. Do not send mixed messages. Simply, ignore the bad behavior and reward your dog when he does the action you request to be done. Teach your dog some simple commands to communicate what you want, such as, "drop it," or "leave it."

- Keep the training sessions short at 15 minutes maximum per session. You will be continuously training your companion, but use the formal training sessions to focus on one objective. Any session longer than 15 minutes will be hard for your dog to stay focused. During training, this is the attention span of most canines. Ten minutes per session is a good time limit for young puppies. Some breeds stay puppies longer than others stay, and may not fully develop until year two. Use a variety and an abundance of different treats and rewards. Rewards are play, toys, praise, affection, treats, and anything that you know that your dog enjoys.

- Run, run, run! It is understood that your dog will be much happier if you run your dog every day. Run your dog until his tongue is hanging out. If he is still full of energy, run him again and he will love you for this. Before a training session begins, use a little exercise to release some of your dog's energy, this can increase his ability to focus during the session. Toy and many small dogs do not require excessive exercise but still require daily walks and play sessions.

- It is very important that you make sure your dog is comfortable in all sorts of situations. All dogs, even your sweet tempered Aire, have the potential to bite. Making sure, he is comfortable in various situations and teaching your dog to be gentle with his mouth will reduce the risk of unwanted bites. Mouthing should not be acceptable behavior because it leads to worse actions.

- Kids are great, are they not? However, the notion that kids and dogs are as natural a pairing as chocolate and peanut butter is simply not true. Kids are often bitten by dogs because they unintentionally do things that frighten dogs. Sometimes a child's behavior appears like prey to a dog. Never leave a dog and a child together unsupervised, even if the dog is *good* with children. Teach children not to approach a dog that is unfamiliar to them. The way a child behaves with the familiar family dog, may not be appropriate with another dog that they meet for the first time. Instruct children that tail pulling, hugging their necks tightly, leg pulling, and hard head pats are not acceptable.

Solving Unwanted Behaviors

How to deal with a problem behavior before it becomes a habit

Everyone likes his or her own space to feel comfy, familiar, and safe. Your dog is no different. A proper living space is a key factor to avoiding all kinds of potential problems. Think of all the things your puppy will encounter in his life with humans. Things like baths, walks, radio, TV, neighbors, visitors, household appliance noises, construction, engines, lawnmowers, and so forth that are not necessarily familiar or common in nature, and can be frightening to your dog. It is essential to use treats, toys, and praise to assist you and your dog while in the midst of training and socializing.

Dogs are social creatures and it is essential to communicate with them. Communication is always the key to behavior reinforcement. Showing your dog that calm behavior is frequently rewarded, and that you have control over his favorite things, acts as a pathway to solving problems that may arise down the road.

Keep your dog's world happy. Make sure he is getting a proper amount of exercise and that he is being challenged mentally. Make sure he is getting enough time in the company of other dogs and other people. Keep a close eye on his diet, offering him good, healthy, dog-appropriate foods. A small treat every now and then is perfectly in order. Avoid excessive helpings when treating.

It is important that you be a strong leader. Dogs are pack animals and your dog needs to know that you are the *alpha*. Do not let situations fall into that questionable "who's the boss?" scenario. Your puppy will feel confident and strong if he works for his rewards and knows that he or she has a strong, confident leader to follow. Let your dog show you good behavior before you pile on the goodies, or a new roof on his doghouse. With a little work on his part, he will appreciate it more.

Getting by the challenges

Your dog's first step towards overcoming the challenges in life is in understanding what motivates his own behavior. Some behaviors your dog will exhibit are instinctual. Chewing, barking, digging, jumping, chasing, digging, and leash pulling are things that all dogs do because it is in their genetic make-up. These natural behaviors differ from the ones we have inadvertently trained into the domestic canine. Behaviors such as nudging our hands asking to be petted, or barking for attention, are actually accidently reinforced by us humans and not innate.

What motivates your dog to do what he does or does not do? You may wonder why he does not come when you call him while he is playing with other dogs. Simply, this may be because coming to you is far less exciting than scrapping with the same species. When calling your dog you can change this behavior simply by offering him a highly coveted treat and after treating, allow him to continue playing for a while. Start this training aspect slowly, and in short distances from where he is playing. Gradually increase the distances and distractions when you beckon your dog.

Here are some helpful tips to use when trying to help your Airedale Terrier through challenging behavior.

- Are you accidentally rewarding bad behavior? Remember that your dog may see any response from you as a reward. You can ignore the misbehavior if you are patient enough, or you can give your puppy the equivalent of a human *time out* for a few minutes. Make sure the time out environment is in a calm, quiet and safe, but very dull place, similar to my grandma's condo in Florida. More on time outs later inside this guide.

- Think about the quality of his diet and health. Is your dog getting enough playtime, mental and physical exercise, and sleep? Is this a medical problem? Do not ignore the range of possibilities that could be eliciting your dog's challenging behavior.

- Be sure and practice replacement behavior. Reward him with something that is much more appealing than the perceived reward that he is getting when he is misacting. It is important to reward his good behavior before he misacts. If done consistently and correctly, this will reinforce good behaviors, and reduce poor behaviors.

For example, in the hopes of receiving love, your dog is repeatedly nudging your hand; teach him to *sit* instead by only giving him love after he sits, and never if he nudges you. If you command, "sit" and he complies, and then you pat him on the head or speak nicely to him, or both, your dog will associate the sitting compliance with nice things. If he nudges and you turn away and never acknowledge him he will understand that behavior is not associated with nice things. In a scenario where your dog is continually nudging you for attention, you want to catch him before he comes running into your room and begins nudging, and then, immediately say, "sit."

- While practicing the replacement behavior, be sure you reward the right response and ignore the mistakes. Remember, any response to the wrong action could be mistaken as a reward by your dog, so try to remain neutral in a state of ignoring, this includes, sight, touch and verbal acknowledgement. Be sure to offer your dog a greater reward for the correct action than the joy he is getting from doing the wrong action. You will have to think up counter actions for each wrong action you are replacing.

- Your dog's bad behavior may be caused by something that causes him fear. If you decipher this as the problem try to change his mind about what he perceives frightening. Pair the scary thing with something he loves. Say your dog has a problem with the local skateboarder. Pair the skateboarder's visit with a super treat and lots of attention. He will soon look forward to the daily arrival of the skateboarder.

- Always, remain patient with your dog and do not force changes. Work gradually and slowly. Forcing behavioral changes on your dog may lead to making the behaviors worse. Training requires that you work as hard as your dog, and maybe harder, because you have to hone your observational skills, intuition, timing, patience, laughter, and the understanding of your dog's body language and demeanor.

Rewards in Lieu of Punishment

It is always better to reward your Airedale instead of punishing him or her. Here are a few reasons why:

- If you punish your dog, it can make him distrust, or cause fear, aggression, and avoidance of you. If you rub your dog's nose his doodie or pee, he may avoid going to the bathroom in front of you. This is going to make his public life difficult.

- Physical punishment has the tendency to escalate in severity. If you get your dog's attention by a light tap on the nose, he will soon get used to that and ignore it. Shortly the contact will become more and more violent. As we know, violence is *not* the answer.

- Punishing your dog may have some bad side effects. For example, if you are using a pinch collar, it may tighten when he encounters other dogs. Dogs are very smart, but they are not always logical. When your dog encounters another dog, the pinching of the collar may lead him to think that the other dog is the reason for the pinch. *Pinch collars have been linked to the reinforcement of aggressive behaviors between dogs.*

- Electric fences will make him avoid the yard.

- Choke collars can cause injuries to a dog's throat as well as cause back and neck misalignment.

- You may inadvertently develop and adversarial relationship with your dog if you punish your dog instead of working through a reward system and correctly leading. If you only look for the mistakes within your dog, this is all you will begin to see. In your mind, you will see a problem dog. In your dog's mind, he will see anger and distrust.

- You ultimately want to shape your dog's incorrect actions into acceptable actions. By punishing your dog, he will learn only to *avoid* punishment. He is not learning to change the behavior you want changed, instead he learns to be sneaky or to do the very minimum to avoid being punished. Your dog can become withdrawn and seemingly inactive. Permanent psychological damage can be done if a dog lives in fear of punishment.

- If you punish rather than reward neither you nor your dog will be having a very good time. It will be a constant, sometimes painful struggle. If you have children, they will not be able to participate in a punishment based training process because it is too difficult, and truly no fun.

- Simply put, if you train your dog using rewards, you and your dog will have a much better time and relationship. Rely on rewards to change his behavior by using treats, toys, playing, petting, affection, or anything else you know your dog likes. If your dog is doing something that you do not like, replace the habit with another by teaching your dog to do something different, and then reward him or her for doing the replacement action, and then you can all enjoy the outcome.

Everything Treats

You are training your puppy and he is doing well, *of course*, because he is the best dog in the world! *Oh yes he is.* Because of this fact, you want to make sure that you are giving your dog the right kind of treats. Treats are easy. As long as you stay away from the things that aren't good for dogs, such as; avocado, onions, garlic, coffee, tea, caffeinated drinks, grapes, raisins, macadamia nuts, peaches, plums, pits, seeds, persimmons, chocolate, whiskey & soda, Guinness Stout, just to name a few.

You can make treats from many different foods. First, treats should be small, kernel sized, and easy to grab from a pocket or concealable container (treat pouches are available). When you are outdoors and there are many distractions, treats should be of a higher quality and coveted by your pooch, we call it a higher value treat because it is worthy of your dog breaking away from the activity he is engaged. Perhaps cubes of cheese, dried meat, special kibble or the neighbor cat (just joking all you cat lovers). Make sure you mix it up and keep a variety of snacks available when you are out and about. Nothing is worse during treat training than your dog or puppy turning his nose up at a treat because he has grown bored of it or it holds a lesser value than something else does that currently interests him.

Here are some treat ideas:

- No sugar, whole grain cereals are good. Cheerios are good choice. There is no need for milk, bowl, or a spoon. You can just give your dog the goods, as is.

- Kibble (dry foods). Put some in a paper bag and boost the aroma factor by tossing in some bacon or another meat product. Dogs are all about those yummy smell sensations.

- Beef Jerky that preferably has no pepper or heavy seasoning.

- Carrot, apple pieces, and some dogs even enjoy melons.

- Baby food meat products. You know the ones, those strange little suspect pink sausage things.

- Commercial dog treats. Be careful, there as there are tons of them on the market. Look for those that do not have preservatives, by products, or artificial colors.

- Cubed meats that are preferably not highly processed or salted.

- Shredded cheese, string cheese or cubed cheese. Dogs love cheese!

- Cream cheese, peanut butter, or spray cheese. Give your dog a small dollop to lick for every proper behavior.

- Ice Cube, Not the rap star but the frozen water treats. Your dog will love crunching these up. . If your dog has dental problems, proceed cautiously.

Avoid feeding your hairy friend from the dining table; because you do not want to teach your dog to beg when people are sitting down to eat. When treating, give treats far from the dinner table or a good distance from where people normally gather to eat.

Providing the Treats

Treats, treats, *treats!* *"Come and get 'em."* How many times have you heard a friend or family member tell you about some crazy food that their dog loves? Dogs do love a massive variety of foods; unfortunately, not all of the foods that they think they want to eat are good for them. Dog treating is not rocket science but it does take a little research, common sense, and paying attention to how your dog reacts after wolfing down a treat.

I am going to throw out some ideas for treats for training as well as some regular ole "Good Dog" treats for your sidekick and friend in mischief. I will touch on the proper time to treat, the act of giving the treat, types of treats, and bribery vs. reward.

Types of Treats

Love and attention is considered a reward and is certainly a positive reinforcement that can be just as effective as an edible treat. Dog treating is comprised of edibles, praise, love, and attention. Engaging in play or allowing some quality time with their favorite piece of rawhide is also effectual. At times, these treats are crucial to dog training.

Human foods that are safe for dogs, include most fruits and veggies, cut up meats that are raw or cooked, yogurt, peanut butter, kibble, and whatever else you discover that your dog likes, but be sure that it is good for him, in particular his digestive system. Remember, not all human foods are good for dogs. Please read up on the dos and don'ts regarding human foods and dogs. A "treat" is considered something about the size of a kernel of corn. All a dog needs is a little taste to keep him interested. The *kernel size* is something that is swiftly eaten and swallowed, making it non-distracting from training. Remember, a treat is just quick tasted, used for enticement and reinforcement.

Giving the Treat

Try to avoid treating your dog when he is over stimulated and running amuck in an unfocused state of mind. This can be counterproductive and might reinforce a negative behavior resulting in you not being able to get your dog's attention.

When giving the treat, allow your dog to get a big doggie whiff of that nibble of tasty food treat, but keep it up and away from a possible attempt at a quick snatch and grab. Due to their keen sense of smell, they will know long before you would that there is a tasty snack nearby. Issue your command and wait for him to obey before presenting the doggie reward. Remember when dog treating, it is important to be patient and loving, but it is equally important not to give the treat until he obeys. Try to use treating to reward the kickback mellow dog, not the out of control or over-excited dog.

Some dogs have a natural gentleness to them and always take from your hand gently, while other dogs need some guidance to achieve this. If your dog is a bit rough during treat grabbing, go ahead and train the command "gentle!" when giving treats. Be firm from this point forward. Give up no treats unless taken gently. Remain steadfast with your decision to implement this, and soon your pup or dog will comply, if he wants the tasty treat.

Time to Treat

The best time to be issuing dog treats is in between his or her meals. During training, always keep the tastiest treat in reserve in case you need to reel in your dog's attention back to the current training session. It is good to keep in mind that treating too close to meal times makes all treats less effective, so remember this when planning your training sessions. Obviously, if your dog is full from mealtime he will be less likely to want a treat reward than if he is a bit hungry, therefore your training session will likely be more difficult and far less effective.

What's In the Treats?

Before purchasing, look at the ingredients on the treat packaging, and make certain there are no chemicals, fillers, additives, colors and things that are unhealthy. Certain human foods that are tasty to us might not be so tasty to your dog, and he will tell you. Almost all dogs love some type of raw or cooked meats. In tiny nibble sizes, these treats work great to get their attention where you want it focused.

Many people like to make homemade treats and that is fine, just keep to the rules we just mentioned and watch what you are adding while you are having fun in the kitchen. Remember to research and read the list of vegetables dogs can and cannot eat, and note that pits and seeds can cause choking and intestinal issues, such as dreaded doggy flatulence. Remove the seeds and pits, and clean all fruits and veggies before slicing it into doggie size treats.

Bribery vs. Reward Dog Treating

The other day a friend of mine mentioned *bribery* for an action when he wanted his dog to shake his hand. I thought about it later and thought I would clarify for my readers. *Bribery* is the act of offering the food in advance to get the dog to act out a command or behavior. *Reward* is giving your dog his favorite toy, food, love, affection *after* he has performed the behavior.

An example of bribery would be, if you want your dog to come and you hold out in front of you in your hand a huge slab of steak before calling him. Reward would be giving your dog the steak after he obeyed the "come!" command.

Bribed dogs learn to comply with your wishes only when they *see* food. The rewarded dog realizes that he only gets his reward after performing the desired action. This also assists by introducing non-food items as rewards when training and treating. Rewards such as play, toys, affection, and praise can be substituted for treats.

About Alpha Dog's

Importance of Leading by Being the Alpha Dog

Having the respect from the entire pack and remaining unchallenged as to whom is the leader of the pack is the goal for all dog trainers and owners. Although there exists evidence that today's dogs are far removed from wolves, wild dogs still respect an alpha leader to follow. The *alpha* wields absolute power. The facts are that dogs thrive under structure and understanding of rule etiquette. They are more relaxed and at ease, if they know that their needs are being met by their alpha leader.

Alpha dogs possess poise, confidence, bravery, intelligence, and self- control. Additionally they tend to be affectionate, making them very good pets. An alpha does not have to be overly strong, savage, or large to be in the power seat. To personify an alpha's attributes, they tend to hold a keen mental fortitude made up of a combination of wisdom, intelligence, and charisma or some combination thereof that makes them good leaders, and allows them to dominate.

Dogs are still the only species that have allowed humans to dominate them. Dogs willingly live with humans and assist us with our lives. We have all heard the saying, "man's best friend since we were children, and of course they are also "women's best friend." This saying truly fits dogs, as they are intelligent enough to take our orders but can also discern if you deserve their respect as alpha of the pack. Many breeds will absolutely challenge humans as alpha if they are not put into their place early. If you pay attention, you will notice that in every family there is one member above all others that the family dog respects. That person is the *alpha*.

Being the alpha keeps you in charge and respected. This allows living with your dog to be an easier and healthier arrangement. Knowing that your dog will listen when necessary, and obey your commands, makes life together less challenging and more rewarding.

Regardless of the breed, your dog is seeking a leader. Giant breeds, your dog, or the "Sir-Barks-A-lot" all need to be controlled and led by an alpha. Yep, even the little micro breed lapdogs needs a commander. Masters needs to guide, care, love, protect, instruct, and show affection to their dogs, furthermore, dogs seek it.

Unfortunately, many dog owners abandon their dogs. Complaints are many and vary widely, but common complaints are that their dog is "not trainable" and that "they will not obey commands." What these dog owners do not realize is that you have to show dogs that you deserve the respect, loyalty, and obedience from them. For the entire population of those seemingly non-trainable, hyperactive, house destroying dogs, there is an owner who was unable to achieve the alpha position and be the leader of the pack.

Dogs need a leader to follow so they can be taught acceptable social behaviors. They are innocent to knowing what behaviors are acceptable until they are taught. Without a leader, they have no direction and act out their own desires. If they do this and are not disciplined they end up with anti-social behavior. Dogs that will be living alongside humans must have an owner capable to be the pack-leading alpha they want to follow.

Who wants to be the Alpha?

Inside your family unit, an *alpha* needs to be chosen to lead your dog and the entire family needs to support this family member in his or her alpha role. In order for your dog to obey and become social, a family member needs to be the alpha your dog admires. An alpha needs to be confident, intelligent, and charismatic for commanding respect. For this reason, the other family members must never undermine your rules for acceptable dog behavior. In a sense, the rest of the family needs to act as though they are in your pack and follow your lead in any dog related activities. *This will establish all humans above your dog in the pecking order.* The other members of the family (think pack), as well as visiting friends and family, will help to reinforce and establish acceptable dog protocol.

As I have mentioned repeatedly, the alpha is the top dog and his word needs to be the final word. This essential concept cannot be emphasized enough. The alpha needs to be above all others in the house. He or she can still show affection, and should. The leader *does not* need to be mean or physically abusive. The pack boss makes rules and is first in everything. It is understood that these rules are final. It should be made clear that the alpha will eat first, drink first, walk through doors first, leads on walks, and so forth. These rules should be adhered by the entire family and all visiting friends, humans are therefore established as above dogs.

Essentially the alpha dog remains calm, consistent, even-tempered, fun loving, and firm but fair throughout training and rule enforcement, while always delivering commands and corrections with the energy of confident authority. Additionally he or she shows love, affection, and reliability towards their dog, and all of these combined gains and keeps the respect of the owner's dog, allowing for a lifetime of joyful harmonious living.

Being the alpha leader means that you are in control and you maintain this control through the power of your mental abilities, *not from your physical responses*. You are there to gently, but firmly lead your dog into the correct direction by shaping his behavior. Whether it is in obedience training or socialization, vigilant and thoughtful leadership will eventually create a happy, joyful life together as your dog's master and friend.

The guidelines to establishing a person as an alpha leader are laid out in my book **"Alpha Dog, Don't Think BE - Alpha Dog - Alpha Dog Training Secrets."**

Terrier Breeds Traits

All dogs come with their own unique individual personalities, but they also carry forward their heredity. Having knowledge of the original breeding purpose, where traits were both bred in and out, helps to offer insight into the characteristics of your particular breed. Those negative and positive behaviors that you might encounter as you are raising, training, and living with your new dog are directly linked to intentional trait manipulation.

Many terrier dog breeds were developed in the United Kingdom with a common and practical focus of locating and killing vermin. Needing to fit into rodent burrows, most terriers tend to be small and lean with a rough wiry coat that requires little maintenance. In addition to their job as rodent exterminators, they were bred for foxhunting, sport, and dog fighting. A result of this specialized breeding, terriers were often pugnacious and aggressive, but over subsequent years, most of these traits have been reduced to a certain extent. Still, most terrier breeds are quite vocal and are inclined to chase moving objects. They also have a fearless demeanor that keeps them from retreating during most confrontations. Many terrier breeds are named from the area in which that particular breed was developed, for example, Norwich, Bedlington, Irish, Border, and Boston. Depending upon who and how they are categorized there an estimated sixty to one-hundred terrier breeds.

Generally, terriers have a low tolerance for other animals, including other dogs. Since terriers were originally bred to hunt, chase, and kill rodents, otters, fox and other animals, their independence and predatory drive persists. This is one of the reasons why many terrier breeds love to dig, because they are used to pursuing and dispatching their prey, often when underground. This residual predatory drive is why furry pets, including cats, will always be in danger of chase and possible attack. Not all, but most terriers have a fearless streak, which often makes them willing and ready to confront other animals, humans not excluded. Usually friendly and enjoying human company, terriers are often reserved around strangers. Terriers are also not the type of breed that is glued to their humans, perpetually under foot. As for fur, many of the terrier breeds carry a wiry coat that requires a grooming technique named stripping to keep the color and fur in proper condition. Stripping pulls the shed hair from the coat and maintains the dogs distinguishing coat texture and color.

With their representative spunk, energy, and stubbornness, owning a terrier normally requires owners to be strong willed and able to maintain, as well as assert their alpha dominance. This essential role of pack leader can only be achieved and maintained through consistent reinforcement, discipline, and ongoing training. It should be noted that not all terriers get along with other dogs, and in general are often considered best suited to be the only family dog. Because of their high energy and playfulness, terriers can make terrific pets if they are properly socialized. Through early socialization, most terriers will get along fine with other dogs, and even with cats. It is important to begin training your terrier puppy at around six to eight weeks, and ongoing throughout their lifetime. Do not forget to exercise vigorously your always abundantly energetic puppy on a daily basis. An absence of exercise can often lead to various negative behavioral and health issues, which can manifest in highly unwanted and destructive behaviors.

Digging and barking can be troublesome with terriers, so it is suggested to correct these issues early using ongoing behavioral modifications and training. A serious digger can prevent you from having a productive garden or a nice plot of lawn, and incessant barking will not only disturb your peace, but that of your neighbors as well. For digging help, you may consider creating a special area, such as a designated digging pit for them to do what they do best. For the canine escape artist, and terriers are masters, proper fencing that extends down into the ground about one foot (30cm), or chicken wire buried deep beneath the soil will help to prevent the potential for a breach.

A talented breed, terriers compete in sports of agility, including lure racing, Frisbee™, and flyball. They are also excellent at scenting, Earthdog trials, which tests their skills as hunters without prey.

Terriers are quick and athletic, and often enjoy accompanying humans while hiking, jogging, or during long walks. They require strong, consistent leadership, and usually respond well to rewards based clicker training. Remember to expect that many of the terrier's strong characteristics will challenge your spot as the alpha, so it is essential to remain diligent in securing and maintaining the role as your dog's leader and provider. Remember to reinforce wanted behaviors with frequent rewards, such as treats, play, and praise. As a part of their breeding, terriers are independent and accustomed to solving problems on their own, so incentives will help you in training. The commands of *stay*, *come*, *leave it*, and *no*, should be taught early.

Terrier Types & Groups

Breed group classifications are not scientific and vary within the different kennel clubs. For example, the Miniature Schnauzer is placed in the Terrier Group by the American Kennel Club but not categorized as Terrier by the Kennel Club (UK), which places all Schnauzers in the Utility Group. Boston Terriers are true terriers although the Kennel Club also places them in the Utility Group, while the Canadian Kennel Club places them in the Non-Sporting Group. The Tibetan Terrier is not a true terrier, and thus only a terrier by name. No matter which group the different terriers are classified, a terrier is still a terrier. In 18th century Britain, terriers were divided into two groups, long and short-legged. Just keep in mind terrier categorization is informal and non-scientific.

Working Terriers

These hunting type terriers are still used to find, track, trail, and hold prey at bay. Many specialize in underground type hunting where they attempt to bolt the prey into the hunter's sights. Some of these are the Jack Russell, Patterdale, Cairn, Scottish, and West Highland White Terrier. All of these types were originally bred and trained to hunt and kill small vermin in barns, homes, and around farms, and if necessary go underground to bolt or kill the prey.

Fell Terriers

These terriers were developed in Northern England and their primary focus was to assist hunters in killing foxes by either bolting the fox from its den or killing it by itself. They are long legged working terriers such as the Patterdale, Lakeland, and Black Fell Terrier, usually weighing less than 15lb (6.5kg), and having narrow chests that enable them to fit into burrow entrances. They are bred strictly for hunting ability and gameness.

Hunting Terriers

These terriers were developed in Southern England and their primary focus was to assist hunters in locating and bolting foxes during traditional mounted foxhunts. Horse oriented social clubs chasing red fox utilize these types of terrier breeds. Some breeds that came from these are the Jack Russell, Plummer, Toy Fox, Fox, and the Brazilian Terriers.

Toy Terriers

These types of terriers were bred down in size from larger terriers with the primary focus of companionship and showing in the Toy category. The Toy Fox, Manchester, Russian Toy, and the Rat Terriers are a few in this category. Although small in stature, they are still terriers in personality and do not enjoy lazing around on their masters laps in the manner true companion dogs often enjoy. Toy terriers retain a strong predatory drive, during hunting they would be carried upon horseback, and released once the prey was near.

Bull type Terriers

These dogs came from crossing Bulldogs and terriers and their original purpose was for sports such as bull baiting, bear baiting, and pit fighting, as well as being used for guarding purposes. As these practices grew out of favor and laws were passed prohibiting these activities, breeders began to make these bull type dogs into easy-going, highly trainable family dogs that could be trusted with children and other animals.

Unfortunately, the underground fighting of these dogs has continued and thrived. This has contributed to an unearned stigma that has grown into anti-bull legislation and demonization of these breeds, such as the American Pit Bull, Bull Terrier, Staffordshire Bull Terrier, and American Staffordshire Terrier. The media has unfairly contributed to this with their sensationalist and often-incorrect coverage of dog attacks. The onus lies with us humans in the mistreatment of these dogs, and with the purposeful breeding of aggressive traits simply to continue with the blood sport of pit dog fighting. These aggressive traits were successfully bred out of these breeds, and with the Staffordshire Terrier for example, who continues to be a beloved family dog that is affectionate, good with children and a trustworthy dog to have in the house.

BEGIN TRAINING
Housetraining

The fact is, dogs are a bit particular about where they "potty" and will invariably build a very strong habit. When housetraining your puppy, remember that whenever he goes *potty somewhere* in the house, he is building a strong preference to that particular area. This is why preventing soiling accidents is very important; additionally thoroughly cleaning the area where the defecation occurred is important.

When your puppy does relieve his self in the house, *blame yourself*. Until your puppy has learned where he is supposed to do his business, you should keep a constant, watchful eye on him, whether he is in his crate, on a mat, beside you, or on the couch. While potty training, some people will *tether* their puppies to their waist or to a nearby object. This allows them to keep their puppies in eyesight.

- When your pup is indoors but out of the crate, watch for sniffing or circling, and as soon as you see this behavior, take him outdoors right away. *Do not hesitate.*

- If your pup is having accidents in the crate, the crate may be too big. The crate should be big enough for your puppy to stand up, turn around, and lie down in. If crate accidents occur, remove any soiled items from the crate and thoroughly clean it.

- Keep your puppy confined to their specific gated puppy area where accidents can be easily cleaned, such as section of bathroom, pantry, laundry, or similar. Do not leave your puppy confined to their crate for hours upon end. You want their crate to be an enjoyable place that they find safe and comforting.

- Set a timer to go off every hour so that you remember to take your puppy out before nature calls. With progress, you can increase the time duration between potty stops. Some Toy dogs need to go more frequently, around every thirty to forty-five minutes.

- If your pup does not do his *duty* when taken outdoors, bring him back indoors and keep a close eye on him. One option is to keep your pup tethered to your waist so that he is always in eyesight, then try again in 10-15 minutes.

- While you are away. If possible, arrange to have a person to take your puppy outside to eliminate.

Establish a Schedule

- You should take your puppy out many times during the day, most importantly after eating, playing, or sleeping. Feed your puppy appropriate amounts of food two or three times per day and leave the food down for around fifteen-minutes at a time, then remove. You can keep a pups water down until about eight at night, but then remove it from your puppy's reach.

- Puppies can generally hold for a good one-hour stretch. Larger breeds of dogs can hold their bladders longer than smaller dog breeds. Some small dogs cannot last the night before needing to go outside. Most adult dogs generally do not go longer than 8-10 hours between needing to urinate.

- Gradually, your puppy will be able to hold urinating for increasingly longer lengths of time, but until then keep to the every hour schedule. Keeping your puppies excrement outdoors, fast tracks your puppy's potty training success.

Consistency Is the Mother of Prevention

Until your puppy is reliably housetrained, bring him outside to the same spot each time, always leaving a little bit of his waste there as a scent marker. This will be the designated potty spot. If you like, place a warning sign at that spot. Remember to use this spot for potty only, and not for play. Bring your puppy to his spot, and when you see him getting ready to go potty, say something like "potty time," "hurry up," or "now." As your pup is going, do not speak because it will distract him. Instead, ponder how much fun it will be when he is playing fetch and running back to you. When your puppy finishes, *praise, pet, give a top-notch treat*, and spend about five minutes playing with him. If he does not go potty, take your pup inside, keep an eye on him, and try again in 10-15 minutes.

If your puppy goes in the house, remember, that it is *your fault*. Maybe you went too quickly. If you see your puppy relieving himself in the wrong spot, quickly bring him outside to the designated potty spot so that he can finish, then when he is done, offer praise for finishing there. If you find a mess, clean it thoroughly without your puppy watching you do it. Use a cleaner specifically for pet stains so that there is no smell or evidence that you have failed him. This way it will not become a regular spot for your puppy and a new regular clean up chore for you.

This Question Rings a Bell: Can I teach my puppy when to tell me when he needs to go out?

- Yes, you can! Hang a bell at dog level beside the door you use to let your dog outdoors. Put some easy cheese or peanut butter on the bell. When he touches it and rings it, immediately open the door. Repeat this every time and take him to the potty spot. Eventually, he will ring the bell without the easy cheese and this will tell you when he needs to go outside. Be careful here, your puppy may start to ring the bell when he wants to go outside to play, explore, or other non-potty reasons. To avoid this, each time he rings the bell, *only* take him out to the potty spot. If he starts to play, immediately bring him in the house.

Small Dogs often take longer time to potty train. I really do not know why, they just do. One way to help is to take them out more often than you would a larger dog. The longest duration I would go without taking a small dog to the potty spot is about 4 hours, and as a puppy maybe forty-five minutes instead of an hour. In addition, many small or toy dogs do well with a litter box. This way, they can go whenever nature calls and whatever the situation is, such as when there is an ice storm outside and they refuse to get their tiny little paws cold. Because many are easily chilled, some small dogs tend to dislike going outside during foul weather, or even cool conditions. Concurrently, we do not enjoy it either.

Teething, Bones and Chew-toys

Teething

Between the third and sixth week your puppy will begin to feel the notorious baby teeth eruption. Puppy teeth are not designed to grind heavy foods, and consist of predominantly small, razor sharp canines and incisors. These new teeth number about twenty-eight, and during this painful and frustrating teething period, puppies will attempt to seek relief on anything within reach that they can clamp their little mouths down on. Later, when the baby teeth fall out and their adult teeth emerge, this will again cause discomfort, further increasing their drive to chew in search of relief. Usually by the end of six months, the intense chewing phase begins to wane. Although some variance exists by breed, adult dogs have forty-two teeth with the molars coming in last at around six to seven months of age.

Puppies are motivated to chew because of the discomfort that comes from teething, as well as to investigate new objects of interest. Chewing is a normal dog behavior that can be steered and directed toward owner approved toys and objects. Dogs certainly love to chew on bones, and they can spend hours gnawing until they feel that they have successfully scoured it clean, sometimes burying it for a later chew session, or solely as a trophy. Wood, bones and toys are some of the objects that occupy a dog during the activity of chewing. Chewing not only provides stimulation and fun, but it serves to reduce a dog's anxiety. It is our job to identify what our puppies can and cannot chew on, while gently establishing and enforcing the rules of chewing. This process begins by providing an ample amount of chew-toys for our puppy.

Chew-toys

A non-edible chew-toy is an object made for dogs to chew that is neither, consumable or destructible. Non-food items eaten by dogs are dangerous and can sometimes seriously harm your dog, so it is imperative to provide high quality and durable chew-toys. Choosing the type of chew-toy will depend upon your dog's individual preferences and chewing ability, so you may have to go through several to find the most appropriate. Some *super chewer* dogs can destroy a rawhide chew in a fraction of the time as others, so your dog's prowess and jaw power will dictate the types of chews that you will want to provide.

Edible chews such as pig ears, rawhide bones, Nylabones®, and other natural chew products are also available and appropriate for your puppy or adult dog. Beware that sometimes edibles can come apart in large chunks or pieces, thus having the potential to be swallowed, or possibly choke a dog. For safety, keep an eye on your dog whenever he is working away on an edible chew. While your puppy is discovering the variety and joy of chewing, take notice of the chews that he enjoys most.

KONG® and Petsafe® make plenty of top quality chew-toys, including those can be stuffed with food, such as kibble or cheese, to hold your dog's interest. KONG® products as well as the Petsafe® Busy Buddy® line are made from natural rubber and have a stellar reputation for durability. Many other brands are available to choose from. When choosing chew-toys, take into consideration whether or not you are purchasing a natural or synthetic product, as well as keep in mind what your pal's preferences are. Usually, anything that you stuff with food will begin a puppy craving for that particular toy, but be aware that is not always the case.

Stuffing Chew-Toys

There are some basic guidelines to follow when using a stuffable chew toy. First, kibble is the recommended foodstuff when filling your puppy's chew-toy. Kibble assists in keeping your puppy at a normal weight, and if this is a concern, you can simply exclude the amount you used in the toy from his normal feeding portion. Secondly, you can use tastier treats, such as cooked meat or freeze-dried liver, but these should be reserved for special rewards. There are plenty of stuffing recipes available, but be cautious about the frequency you treat your puppy with special stuffing. Be conscious of when you reward your puppy, and avoid doing so when bad behaviors are exhibited. For example, if your puppy has been incessantly barking all afternoon, then if you provide a stuffed chew-toy do not reward him with something utterly delectable.

The art to stuffing chew-toys is that the toy holds your puppy's interest, and keeps him occupied. For your success, you will want to stuff the toy in a way that a small portion of food comes out easily, thus quickly rewarding your puppy. After this initial jackpot, the goal is to keep your puppy chewing while gradually being rewarded with small bits of food that he actively extracts. You can use a high value treat, such as a piece of meat stuffed deeply into the smallest hole, which will keep your dog occupied for hours in search of this prized morsel. With a little creativity and practice, the art of chew-toy stuffing will be acquired benefitting you and your canine friend. After trial and error, you will begin to understand what fillings and arrangements will keep your puppy occupied for longer and longer times.

Why Feed Dinner from Stuffed Chew-Toys?

Here is some advice that I gleaned off a friend of mine, and it does seem to pack some merit. As you are probably aware, the current practice indicates that puppies should be fed two to three times daily, from their bowl. There is nothing wrong with this, but it does raise a question as to whether perhaps they think that they are being rewarded for the non-acceptable behaviors that was possibly acted just prior to eating time. This should be taken into consideration, and feeding should be adjusted to avoid potential negative behavior reinforcement. The other item that I was made aware is that if you feed your puppy by stuffing his chew-toy, it will occupy more of his time and keep him from negatively acting out of boredom, excessive curiosity, or abundant adrenal stores.

The argument against bowl feeding is that it supplants the activity of searching for food, as they would in the wild, and as a result of the quick gratification in the easy meal, there remains an over-abundance of time remaining to satisfy the dog's mental and physical stimulation. To understand this better you have to put yourself into a puppy's paws. Besides sleeping and training, your dog has about twelve hours each day to fill with satisfying and rewarding activity. Resulting from an excess of unoccupied time, normal behaviors, such as grooming, barking, chewing, walking, and playing can become repetitive and unfulfilling. Sometimes an activity can lose its initial purpose and meaning, only to become a way to pass time instead of serving as a positive function of daily life. Obsessive and compulsive behaviors can come out of these long sessions of boredom. For example, vocalizing for alarm can become ceaseless barking, and grooming can turn into excessive licking or scratching, likely resulting in harm to the skin.

It falls upon us to instruct our puppies on healthy, calm and relaxing ways to pass the time of day. This is a critical part of training and socialization. Remember, that by stuffing the chew-toy full of kibble you can successfully occupy hours of your puppy's time, helping to reduce the possibility of negative behaviors overtaking your puppy. This can be accomplished by redirecting his attention to an activity that he enjoys, keeping his mind distracted from the potential of loneliness and boredom. Because of his time spent chewing the approved toy, he is kept calm and his time occupied, periodically rewarded by bits of kibble, and thus the possibility of developing any of the potential, aforementioned negative behaviors is minimized.

This feeding option is a method originally suggested by Dr. Ian Dunbar, a famed rewards-based trainer and SIRIUS® puppy-training pioneer. However, this method is not essential to maintain and train a healthy puppy; I felt it was worth mentioning since I was writing about chew-toys. Many people refrain from feeding their dog's kibble, utilizing the optional diet of raw foods, thus modification in the feeding method would be required here. Other factors when utilizing this method should take into consideration your dog's individual personality, as well as ability to withdraw food from the toy. Whichever feeding method you choose to use, be certain to feed your puppy the healthiest, least processed, non-chemical laden foods that you can find.

Bones

Later, as your puppy grows he will no doubt be interested in other types of things to chew on, as well as to eat. There exists some controversy as to whether raw bones, cooked bones, or any animal bones are at all good for dogs to chew. I do not want to state with certainty that bones are safe for your dog, as there is some obvious risks involved, but I do feed my dogs bones without problem. As a new dog owner, and with time and assessment, you can later determine what is best for your dog. Any concerns that surface can be solved by consulting your veterinarian, speaking with your breeder, and of course making a decision based upon your own findings and personal experience.

Recommendations are to provide your dog with bones that are sold specifically for chewing, which are often beef, or bison femur or hipbones, filled with satisfying marrow. Chicken bones and steak bones that have been cooked can splinter and pose a greater choking risk and should not be given to your dog. Some dogs that are intense chewers often chip a tooth, or splinter small pieces off the bones they are gnawing at, and because of this, it is good to supervise them. Be sure to avoid small bones in favor of larger raw bones. Present the bones on an easy to clean surface or somewhere outdoors. If you have more than one dog, it is important to separate them to avoid conflict. Also, be aware that dogs not who are not used to the rich, high calorie marrow inside of these bones could possibly have a bout of diarrhea after consumption.

Chew-toy Training

This is an option to controlling and shaping the chewing behavior. Something that I learned from other trainers is how to establish a chew-toy obsession for your puppy. When you bring your puppy home, you should immediately begin exposing him to chew-toys, always keeping them in close proximity, so you can effectively steer all of his chewing energies into these toys instead of your expensive leather shoes, flip-flops, or comfy slippers. Puppies love to chew on just about anything that they can get their mouths on, but depending upon your puppy's personality there exists some variance in the frequency and ferocity of the chewing. There is no reason to leave it to chance. By establishing an early obsession to chew-toys, you can be assured that all of your valuable human articles will be spared from the chewing machines we call *puppies.* As the owner of a new puppy, you will want to thoroughly puppy-proof your home. Until he has completely learned that his toys are the only acceptable objects for him to chew, everything in your house should be considered *at risk.*

Chew-toys provide puppies a focal point in which to channel their energy, and serve to keep boredom from setting up shop. It is a necessity to teach your puppy early on that the chew-toys you provide are fun and delicious. A good way to do this is to take advantage of the hollow toys, and stuff them with kibble, or other tasty treats of your choice. To bolster this training, you can keep your puppy's food bowl hidden for the first few weeks after his arrival, and serve all of your puppy's kibble from the stuffed toy, or a sterilized bone. Taking this action will support your puppy's quick understanding and connection between good things and his chew-toys. Remember, the goal here is to create an obsession to chew-toys, resulting in a dog that will leave all of the other non-chew toy items alone.

In order to reinforce his chew-toy obsession, you can use what is called, *the confinement program.* Through a process in which you narrow the choices of items your dog has available to chew, your puppy eventually will find a kind of solace in his own chew-toys. His association with his own chew-toys will grow as he grows, ultimately resulting in him craving to chew only his chew-toys, and nothing else.

The confinement program training begins by securing your puppy behind his gated area and providing him with plenty of chew-toys to occupy his alone time. Whether you do this prior to leaving the house or while you are in the house, do not forget to leave fresh water for your puppy. Additionally, every hour when you let your puppy out to relieve himself, begin to introduce chew-toy games. There a variety of games you can play, such as find the *hidden chew-toy, chew-toy tug-o-war,* and *fetch.* These games will reinforce his attachment to his chew-toys, and help create a positive obsession toward them. By providing your puppy with a singular choice that is stuffed with food, he will eventually develop a strong chew-toy obsession.

After your dog has formed his chew-toy habit, and has not had any other chewing mishaps, you can broaden his world by expanding his available confinement space to two rooms. As he proves his compliance as evidenced by not chewing items beyond his chew-toys, you can expand his roaming range of access to other rooms in the house, while gradually working up his access to the entire house.

If your puppy makes a chewing mistake, then return to the puppy confinement for 3-6 weeks, all depending upon his progress and the success of further confinement training. After a 3-week period, you will want to test the results of the behavioral modifications resulting from his confinement program. Grant him more access and see if your puppy has reverted to chewing objects on your *no chew list,* or if the program has been a success and it is time move on and enlarge his range. If he reverts again to chewing on objects other than his chew-toys, continue the confinement for a couple of more weeks then test again.

Because this training will be concurrently trained with housetraining, you will also need to monitor if, and when your puppy is having house-soiling accidents. Because your puppy is having accidents indoors, this may limit the house access that you can provide your puppy. It is recommended that in order for you to begin expanding his indoor range of access, your dog should be successfully housetrained, and beyond the possibility of a soiling accident. This training should not conflict with your house-training.

The benefits of making your dog's chew-toys and obsession is more than just for preventing household destruction. It also reduces barking and keeps him from running around the house, because while your puppy is chewing he is distracted, and thus unable to perform other activities. Another potential behavior issue that has negative implications is the separation anxiety that can occur because of your absence. Because chewing occupies your puppies down time, it assists in the prevention and development of separation anxiety. It acts like a blanket or a teddy bear to a child. Furthermore, it is pointed out that a chew-toy addiction is good for dogs that have Obsessive Comive Disorder. This addiction offers them an acceptable avenue to work out their obsessive compulsions. It is not a cure but instead a therapeutic device that can be used by them to obsess.

"Is this a good obsession for my puppy?"

Yes, it is, and additionally a good habit that is difficult to break. The benefits are that your puppy will not be chewing your personal items, and it works well towards keeping him away from compulsive behaviors, such as barking, digging, howling, anxiety from being alone, and a list of other undesirable behaviors. The action of chewing also has a calming benefit, thus acts as a stress reliever. It turns out that a simple rubber chew-toy is an effective tool for controlling and shaping behaviors, as well as a therapeutic tool to occupy and sooth.

Clicker Response Training

Important - *Conceal the treat!* <u>Do not show your puppy the treat before depressing the clicker button,</u> and never deliver the treat prior to the clicker emitting a clicking sound. If you do this, your puppy will be responding to the treat and not the click, and this will undermine your training strategy.

Training should begin by simply observing your Aire puppy. What you are looking for is a desired behavior to reward. In other words, if your puppy is doing anything considered as an undesirable behavior, then do not reward. As long as your puppy is relaxed and behaving well, you can begin to train using this clicker response training. What you are doing here is training your puppy to associate the clicker sound with doing something good. Whenever you click, your puppy will associate the sound with an acceptable performance, and will know that he or she has a reward coming.

Timing is crucial when training your puppy. The essential technique when training your puppy with the clicker is by clicking precisely as the correct action takes place, followed by treating. It does not take long for your puppy to associate their behavior with the clicking sound, and subsequent receiving of a treat. Make sure that the treat is produced *immediately* following the clicking sound.

Note: Throughout this training guide, *Click and Treat is sometimes written as C/T.* In addition, for ease of writing, I refer to the gender of your dog in the male form, even though I know many people have female dogs. Please take no offense to this.

Crucial – *Never click without treating, and never treat without clicking. This maintains the connection and* *continuity between clicking and treating, which is the framework for achieving your desired outcomes.*

Steps

1. When your puppy is relaxed, you should stand, or kneel down at about an arm's length away, then click and give your puppy a treat.

2. Repeat this clicking and treating about 5-15 times. Pause a few seconds between clicks to allow your puppy to resume whatever he was doing. Do not click and treat if he seems to be begging for another treat. Find times throughout the day when he is performing a desired behavior, then click and treat. This teaches your puppy to associate the click with what you want him to do, and a tasty food treat.

When you click, and your puppy's head swings around in anticipation of a treat, then you know that your puppy has made the association between the clicking sound and a reward.

4. Repeat steps one and two the day following the introduction of clicker training. When your puppy quickly responds to the click, then you can begin using the clicker to train commands.

Teaching puppies to respond to this method can take several training sessions, but most commonly after about a dozen click and treats, they begin to connect the clicking sound with a treat. Usually, at the end of the first 5-minute session, puppies tend to swing their head around when they hear the clicker sound.

HELPFUL HINT: After some dedicated training sessions, puppies tend to stop in their tracks and instantly come to you for a treat. At this time refrain from using this clicker technique to get your dog to *come* to you, but instead follow the instructions for teaching the "come" command.

Name Recognition

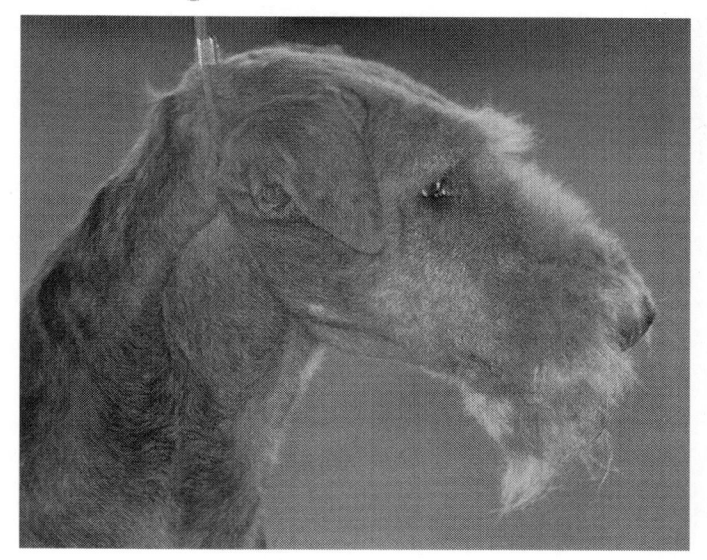

After your puppy responds to the clicking sound, and he knows very well that treats follow the clicking sound, you can now begin teaching him commands and tricks. Now, we are going to teach your puppy some specific things. Let's start with the base exercise that is teaching your puppy to respond to his or her *name*. I assume that you have already gone through the painstaking process of naming your puppy, and now when his or her name is spoken you want your puppy to learn to respond. This can be easy, fun, and satisfying when you finally get positive results.

Teaching your puppy his name is a basic and necessary objective that must be accomplished in order to gain and keep your puppies attention during further training.

Before beginning training, be sure to gather an ample variety of treats. Put these treats in your pockets, treat pouch, or on a tabletop out of sight, and out of your puppy's reach.

1. Ignore your puppy until he looks directly at you, when he does, *click and treat* him. Repeat this 10-15 times. This teaches your puppy to associate the click with a treat, when he looks in your direction.

2. Next, when your puppy looks at you, begin adding your puppy's name, spoken right before you *click and treat*.

3. Continue doing this until your puppy will look at you when you say his or her name.

4. Gradually phase out clicking and treating your puppy every time that he or she looks at you. Decrease C/T incrementally; one out of two times, then one out of three, four, and then not at all. Try not to phase out the C/T too quickly.

After successful name recognition training, you should C/T on occasion, to refresh your puppy's memory and reinforce the association to hearing his name, and receiving a treat. Observe your puppy's abilities and pace during this training process, and adjust appropriately, when needed. The ultimate goal is to have your puppy obey all the commands via vocal or physical cue, *without a reward*.

Responding to his or her name is the most important learned behavior, because it is the base skill of all future training. Therefore, you will want to give this training a considerable amount of attention, and thoroughly complete before moving on.

I advise that you repeat this exercise in various locations around your home, while he is out on the leash, outside in the yard, or in the park. Eventually, make sure that you practice this while there are distractions, such as when there are guests present, when his favorite toys are visible, when there is food around, and when he is among other dogs. Always maintain *good eye contact* when you are calling your puppy's name. Keep on practicing this name recognition exercise until there is no doubt that when you speak your puppy's name, he or she knows whom you are referring to, and they respond appropriately.

It may sound odd, but also try the training when you are in different physical positions, such as sitting, standing, kneeling or lying down. Mix it up so that he gets used to hearing his name in a variety of areas and situations, and repeat this process frequently. No matter the situation, this command *must* be obeyed.

Name recognition will avoid trouble later on down the line. For example, if your puppy gets into something that he should not, such as a scrap with another dog, chasing a cat or squirrel, or far worse, getting involved in a time-share pyramid scheme, you can simply call your puppy's name to gain his attention and then redirect him. You invariably want your puppy to come no matter what the distraction, so training "come" is also a crucial command to teach, and regularly practice throughout the lifetime of your dog. Remember, your puppy first needs to know his or her name so that you can teach these other commands.

To be certain that you are able to grab your dog's attention in any circumstance or situation, continue to practice this training into adulthood to reinforce the behavior. When your puppy is appropriately responding to his or her name, I recommend moving forward to the "come" command.

"Sit"

"Sit" is one of the basic commands that you will use regularly during life with your dog. Teaching your Airedale to *sit* establishes human leadership by shaping your dog's understanding of who the boss is. This command can also help curb problem behaviors, such as jumping up on people. It can also assist in teaching polite doggy etiquette, particularly of patiently waiting for you, *the trusted alpha*. Teaching your dog to sit is easy, and a great way for you to work on your catalog of essential alpha behaviors touched upon in previous chapters.

- First, gather treats, then find a quiet place to begin the training. Wait until your puppy sits down by his own will, and soon as his fuzzy rump hits the floor, *click and treat*. Treat your pup while he is still sitting, then promptly get him up and standing again. Continue doing this until your pup immediately sits back down in anticipation of the treat. Each time he complies, be sure to click and treat.

- Next, integrate the verbal command of "sit." Each time he begins to sit on his own, say, "sit," then reinforce with a C/T. From here on, only treat your pup when he sits after being commanded to do so. Practice for 10-15 repetitions then take a break.

Try these variations for better sitting behavior:

- Continue the training by adding the distraction of people, animals, and noises to the sessions. As with the come command, you want your dog to sit during any situation that may take place. Practice for at least five minutes each day in places with increasingly more distractions.

- Run around with your dog while you are sharing play with one of his favorite toys. After getting him worked up and excited, command your dog to *sit*. Click and treat your dog when he does.

- Before going outside, delivering food, playing with toys, giving verbal praise, petting, or getting into the car, ask your dog to *sit*. Having your dog sit before setting his food bowl down is something you can practice every day to help bolster his compliance to the sit command.

- Other situations where you can practice the sit command can be when there are strangers present, or before opening doors for visitors. In addition, other excellent opportunities to work on the sit command is when there is food on the table, when you are barbequing, or when you are together in the park.

Keep practicing this command in all situations that you may encounter throughout the day with your dog. I recommend a gradual increase to the level of distraction exposure during this training. Sit is a powerful and indispensable command that you will utilize throughout the life of your dog. Later, we will add the command of "sit-stay" in order to keep your dog in place until you release him.

-It is important eventually to phase out the clicking and treating every time that he obeys the "sit" command. After his consistent obedience to the command, you can begin gradually to reduce C/T by treating every other compliance, then once out three times, followed by once out of four, five, six, and then finally cease. Be sure to observe your dog's abilities and pace, making sure not to decrease C/T too rapidly. The overall goal of this training is to have your dog obey all commands without a reward, and only by a vocal or physical cue.

-Take advantage of each day, and the multiple opportunities you have to practice the sit command.

"Come"

After your puppy recognizes, and begins responding to his name being called, then the "come" command takes priority as the first command to teach. *Why?* Because this one could save his life, save your sanity, and avoid you the embarrassment of running through the neighborhood in the middle of the night wearing little more than a robe and slippers, pleading for your dog to return.

If by chance, he is checking out the olfactory magic of the trash bin, the best way to redirect your dog is firmly command him to *"come,"* followed immediately by a reward when he complies. Petting, verbal praise, or play is an appropriate reinforcement and an effective redirecting incentive during this type of situation.

In order to grab your dog's attention, no matter what activity he is engaged in, it is necessary to implement an effective verbal command. Unfortunately, the word *"come"* is a commonly used word that is spoken regularly during daily life, thus making it difficult to isolate as a special command word, so I suggest that a unique and infrequently used word be chosen for this. With my dog Axel, I use "jax" as my replacement word for *come*. For example, I say "Axel *jax*," which replaces the standard, "Axel *come*," or "Axel *here*." When your dog hears this special cue word, he will recognize it as the word associated with the command to return to you and receive a special treat. However, there is nothing wrong with simply using "come" as your command word if you find it effective and natural.

Note: Choose a command word with one or two syllables, and one that you can easily say, because it will be difficult to change the substituted "come" command word later.

Here's what to do-

- If you have chosen to use a unique "come" command, you can begin here. We will not use the clicker at this time. First, gather your assortment of treats, such as bits of steak, bacon, kibble, cheese, or whatever your dog covets most. Start with the tastiest treat in hand, and speak the new command word, immediately followed by a treat. When your dog hears this new word, he will begin to associate it with a special treat. Keep repeating this exercise, and mix up the treats that you provide. Remember to conclude each training session by providing a lot of praise to your dog. Repeat for about ten repetitions then proceed onto the next step.

- Think *treats*. Gather your clicker and treats, and then find a quiet, low distraction place so that both of you can focus. First, place a treat on the floor and walk to the other side of the room. Next, hold out a hand with a visible treat in it. Now, say your dog's name to get his attention, followed by the command "come." Use a pleasant, happy tone when you do this. When your dog begins to move towards you, press the clicker, and praise him all the way to the treat in your hand. The objective of this is for him to ignore the treat on the ground and come to you. When he gets to you, *treat* him from your hand and offer some more praise and affection. Be sure and not click again, only give the treat.

Each time your dog comes to you, pet or touch his head and grab a hold of his collar before treating. Sometimes do this on top of the collar, and sometimes beneath his head on the bottom of the collar. This action gets your dog used to being held, so when you need to grab a hold of him by the collar he will not shy away or fight you.

Do this 10-12 times, and then take a break. Make sure that your dog accomplishes the task by walking the complete distance across the room to you, while wholly ignoring the treat that you placed on the floor.

- For the next session, you will need the assistance of a family member. First, situate yourselves at a distance of about 5-6 paces opposite each other, and place a treat on the floor between the two of you. Each of you show your dog a treat when you say his name followed by "come." Now, take turns calling your dog back and forth between the two of you. Treat and praise your dog each time he successfully comes all of the way to either of you, *while ignoring the treat*. Repeat this about a dozen times. The objective of this exercise is to reinforce the idea that coming when commanded is not only for you, but is beneficial to him as well.

- This time, grab your clicker. As before, put a treat on the ground, move across the room, and then call your dog's name to get his attention, but this time hold out an empty hand and give the command. This will mess with him a little, but that's okay, he's learning. As soon as he starts to come to you, give him praise and when he reaches you, *click and treat* by using the opposite hand that you were luring him. If your dog is not completing the distance to you, press the clicker as he begins to move closer to you, and the first time he completes the distance, give him a supersized treat serving (7-10 treats). Each additional time your dog comes all of the way to you; reward your dog with a regular sized treat serving. Do this about a dozen times, and then take a break.

- Keep practicing this exercise, but now call your dog using an empty hand. Using this technique over several sessions and days should eventually result in a successful hand signal command. Following your dog's consistent compliance with this hand signal training, you can then take the training to the next step by phasing out the hand signal by using only a verbal cue. When shifting to the verbal cue training, reduce treating incrementally, first by treating one out of two times, then one out three times, followed by one out of four, five, six, and lastly without treating at all.

Note: It is important to treat your dog periodically in order to reinforce the desired behavior that he is exhibiting, as well as complying with the command you are issuing. Make sure your dog is coming when commanded; this includes all family members and friends. By the end of this section, your dog should consistently be obeying the hand signal and the verbal "come" commands successfully.

Let's get complex

- Now, by adding distractions we will begin to make obeying commands a more difficult task for your dog. The outcome of this training should result in better control over your pooch in times when there is distracting stimulus.

First, find somewhere where there are sights, sounds, and even smells that might distract your dog. Just about anything can serve as a distraction here. You can intentionally implement distractions, such as having his favorite toy in hand, by having another person present, or even doing this training beside the half of roast ox that is on the rotisserie in the back yard. Indoors, distractive aspects of daily home life, such as cooking, the noise of the television, the doorbell, or friends and family coming and going can serve as distractions. Even move to calling your dog from different rooms of the house, meanwhile gradually introducing other distractions such as music from the stereo, groups of people and combinations of the sort. Of course, the outdoor world is a megamall of potential interruptions, commotions and interferences for your pal to be tantalized and diverted by.

~ During this training exercise, I find it helpful to keep a log of not only how your dog is progressing, but also accounting for the different amounts and kinds of distractions your dog encounters.

Now, in the high stimulus setting, resume training using the previous set of learned commands. As before, begin with treats in hand, because in this instance the snacks will act as a lure for your dog to follow in order to help him focus, rather than as a reward. The goal is to dispense with the treats by gradually phasing them out, eventually only using the vocal command.

When outdoors, you can practice calling the command "come" when you and your dog are in the yard with another animal or person, followed by increasing and more complex distractions. Such as a combination of a person and animal together, then with multiple people conversing or while children are running around, and then you can even throw some toys or balls into the mix. Eventually, move out onto the streets and sidewalks, introducing an even more busy location, remembering to keep track of your dog's progress as the situations become more and more distracting. The goal is that you want your dog to come every time you call "come," no matter how much noise and movement is happening around him.

If your dog begins to consistently return to you seven or eight times out of each ten commands, regardless of the distractions, this shows that the two of you are making very good progress, and that you are well on your way to the ideal goal of nine out of ten times compliant. If your dog is sporting ten out of ten times, you may consider enrolling him at an Ivy League university, or paying a visit to NASA, because you've got yourself one special canine there.

We all want that dog that comes when you use the "come" command. Whether he is seven houses down the road, or just in the next room, a dog that comes to you no matter what he is engaged in, is a dog worth spending the time training.

Interrupting Fetch Exercises, Hide & Seek, and the Decoy Exercise

Practice all of the following exercises with increasing distractions, both indoors and outdoors. Focus on practicing one of these exercises per session, eventually mixing up the order of the exercises as your dog masters each. Remember it is always important to train in a safe area.

- Interrupting Fetch Exercises

Get an ample-sized handful of your Aires favorite treat. Then, lob a ball or a piece of food at a reasonable distance, and as your dog is in the process of chasing it, call him by issuing the *come* command. If he comes *after* he gets the ball/food, give your dog a little reward of one piece of treat. If he comes *before* he gets the ball/food, give your dog a supersized (7-10) serving of treats.

If your dog is not responding to your "come" command, then throw the ball and quickly place a treat down towards his nose height while at the same time saying, "come", when he comes to you click and supersize treat your dog. Then, begin phasing out the treat lure.

After you have thrown the ball/food over several sessions, it is time to change it up. Like the exercise prior, this time you will fake throwing something, and then call your dog. If your dog goes looking for the ball/food before he comes back to you, give a small treat. If he comes immediately after you say, "come," give the supersized treat portion. Repeat this exercise 7-10 times.

- *Hide & Seek*

While you are both outside, and your dog is distracted and does not seem to know you exist, quickly *hide* from him. When your dog comes looking for you, and eventually finds you, *click and treat* your dog in addition with lots of love and praise. By adding a little drama, make it seem like an extremely big deal that your dog has found you. This is something that you can regularly practice and reward.

- *The Decoy*

One person calls the dog; we will call this person the *trainer*. One person tries to distract the dog with food and toys; we will call this person the *decoy*. After the trainer calls the dog, if the dog goes toward the decoy, the decoy person should turn away from the dog and neither of you offer rewards. When the dog goes towards the trainer, he should be rewarded by *both* the trainer and the decoy. Repeat 7-10 times.

HELPFUL HINTS

- Let your dog know that his coming to you is always the best thing ever, sometimes offering him a supersized treat rewards for this behavior. Always reward by treating or praising, and when appropriate you can add play with a favorite toy or ball.

- Never, call your Aire for something he might find unpleasant. To avoid this disguise the real purpose. If you are leaving the field where he has been running, call your dog, put on the leash, and play a little more before leaving. If you are calling your dog to get him into the bath, provide a few minutes of affection or play instead of leading him straight into the bath. This will pacify and distract from any negative association with coming to you.

- You are calling, and your puppy is not responding. What do you do now? Try running backwards away from your dog, crouch, and clap, or show your dog a toy or food. When he comes, still reward him even if he has stressed you out. Running *towards* your dog signals to play *catch me*, so avoid doing this.

- If your dog has been enjoying some unabated freedom off lead, remember to give him a C/T when he checks in with you. Later you can phase out the C/T and only use praise.

- You should practice "come" five to ten times daily, ongoing for life. This command is one of those potentially life-saving commands that helps with all daily activities and interactions. The goal is that your dog will come running to you, whether you are in or out of sight, and from any audible distance. As owners, we know that having a dog that obeys this command makes dog things less stressful.

"Drop it"

Teaching your Airedale to *drop it* is very important. *Why?* Well, if you have ever had a young puppy, you know that it is one giant mouth gobbling up whatever is in sight. Rumor has it that Stephen Hawking actually got the idea of the black hole from his puppy's ever-consuming mouth. Joking aside, sometimes valuable and dangerous things go into that mouth, and the command to "drop it" may save your family heirloom, over even perhaps your dog's life.

If you teach your dog correctly, when you give the command "drop it," he will open his mouth and drop whatever is in there. Most importantly, he will not only drop the item, but he will allow you to retrieve it without protest. When teaching the *drop it* command you must offer a good trade for what your dog has in his mouth. You need to *out-treat* your dog by offering a better treat of higher value in exchange for what he has in his mouth. In addition, it is a good idea to stay calm and not to chase your puppy, as this elicits a play behavior that can work against your desired training outcomes.

If this command is successfully taught, your puppy will actually enjoy hearing "drop it." This command will also build trust between the two of you. In example, if you say, "drop it," then you retrieve the item, and afterward you give a treat, he will know that you are not there simply to steal the thing he has found. Because of the trust that will develop, he will not guard his favorite toys, or food. Negative behaviors, such as guarding, can be avoided with this, and socialization types training.

Teach "Drop It" Like This

- Gather a variety of good treats, the top-shelf stuff, and a few items your dog might like to chew on, such as a favorite toy, or a rawhide chewy. With a few treats in hand, encourage your dog to chew on one of the toys. When the item is in his mouth, *put a treat close to his nose* and say, "drop it!" As soon as he opens his mouth, *click and treat* him as you pick up the item. Then, return the item to your dog.

At this point, your dog may not want to continue to chew on the item because there are treats in the area, and his mouth is now free to consume. If he appears now to be distracted by the treats you possess, rather than the chewy toy, you can take this as an opportunity to pause the training. Be sure and keep the treats handy though, because throughout the day when you see him pick something up, you both can practice the *drop it* command. Do this at least ten times per day, or until this command becomes another command feather in his cap.

In the event that he picks up a forbidden item, like Uncle Clumpy's wooden leg, you may not want to give it back to him. Remember, give your puppy an extra tasty treat, or a supersized serving as an equitable exchange for the peg leg you may have happened to confiscate. You want your puppy to be redirected, and he should be properly rewarded for his compliance.

- Once you have done the treat-to-the-nose *drop it* command ten times, try doing it *without* holding the treat to his nose. Continue to use your hand, but this time it should be empty. Say the command, and when he drops the item, *click and treat*. Make sure the first time he drops it, when you are holding a treat to his nose, that you give him a supersized treat serving from a different hand. Practice this over a few days and training sessions. Do not rush to the next step until his response is consistently compliant, and training is successful.

- This next part of the drop it training will further reinforce the command, in particular during situations where a tug-of-war between you may ensue. This time you will want to use a treat that your dog might find extra special, like a hard chew pig ear or rawhide, making sure that it is something that cannot be consumed quickly. Next, hold this new chewy in your hand and offer it to your dog, but this time *do not let it go*. When your dog has the chewy in his mouth, say, "drop it." When your dog drops it for the *first time*, C/T, being sure to give your dog extra treats, and then offer the chew back to him to keep.

Because better treats are available, he may not take the chewy back. Recognize this as a good sign, but it also signals a time for a break. Later, repeat this training about a dozen times before you move on to the next phase of "drop it." If your dog is not dropping it after clicking, then the next time use a higher value treat.

- For the next phase of the "drop it" command training, repeat the exercise above, but this time do not hold onto the chew, just let him have it. As soon as your dog has it in his mouth, give the command "drop it." When your dog drops the chewy, C/T a supersized portion, then be sure to give the chew back to him to keep. Your dog will be thrilled by this exchange. Once you have successfully done this a dozen times, move onto the next step.

During this exercise, if your dog does not drop the chewy, it will be necessary to show the treat first, as incentive. Once he realizes that you hold treats, you will want to work up to having him drop it before the treat is given. This in actuality is *bribery*, and I do not suggest utilizing this action as a short cut elsewhere during training. *Remember,* only use this method as a last resort, and discontinue it quickly when you do. - Try this command with the things around the house that he is not supposed to chew on, such as pens, chip bags, socks, gloves, tissues, your shoes, or that 15th century Guttenberg bible.

After you and your dog have achieved success indoors with this command, try the exercise outside where there are plenty of distractions. To hold his attention when you are moving into further distracting situations, be sure and have with you the best of treats. Keep in mind that your goal is to have the drop it command obeyed in any situation.

- Practice the drop it command when playing fetch, and other games. For example, when your dog returns to you with his ball, command "drop it," and when he complies, offer up the magic duo of praise, plus a treat.

- Gradually phase out the clicking and treating of your dog every time that he drops something on command. Progressively reduce treating by first treating one out of two times, then one out three times, followed by one out of four, five, six, and finally not at all. Always remain aware of your dog's abilities, and his individual pace, being sure not to decrease treating too rapidly. The desired outcome of this training is that your dog will obey *all* commands by a vocal or physical cue, without a reward.

Know These Things-

- If your Aire already likes to try to incite games of grab and chase with you, it is best to curb this behavior from the onset by teaching your dog that you *will not* chase after him if he thieves and bolts. If your dog grabs and runs, *completely* ignore him. For you to be effective here, it means that you do not indicate your disapproval with any sort of eye contact, body language, or vocalization. He will quickly get bored, and drop the item on his own.

- If your dog refuses to drop an item, you may have to retrieve it manually. You can do this by placing your hand over the top of your dog's muzzle, and with your index finger and thumb placed on either side of his upper lip, firmly pinch it into his teeth. Before utilizing this technique, it is best to attempt to calm your dog's excitement as much as possible. In most cases, your dog will open its mouth to avoid the discomfort, and at this time, you can retrieve the item, whatever it may be. This may take a couple of practices to get the correct pressure and the most effective location to apply it. In the rare instance that this fails, you can simply use both hands and try to separate the jaws by slowly pulling, *not jerking*, the upper and lower jaws apart. Think crocodile handler, minus the severed limbs.

-Another trick for distracting your puppy's attention is by rapping your knuckles on a hard surface, emulating a knock at the door. Often, a puppy will want to investigate what he perceives as a guests arrival, thus dropping whatever is in his mouth to greet the nonexistent visitor.

"Leave it"

Keep in mind that leave it and drop it are distinctly different commands. The goal of the leave it command is to get your Airedale's attention away from any object before it ends up in his mouth. A proficiency in this command will help to keep him safe from dangerous items, for example objects such as dropped medications, broken glass, splintering bones, wires, chemical tainted rags, or that model of the Titanic that you are meticulously working on. Even all of those smelly, frequently dead things that dogs find irresistible and often bring to us as offerings of love and affection, can be thwarted with a simple "leave it." We all know that our dogs love to inspect, smell, taste, and in some cases roll in what they find. You can begin to teach the leave it command as soon as your dog recognizes his own name.

- Start with a treat in each fisted hand. Let him have a sniff of one of your fists. When he eventually looks away from the fist and has stopped trying to get the treat, click and treat, but treat your dog from the opposite hand that he sniffed. Repeat this exercise until he completely refrains from trying to get the treat from you, as evidenced by showing no interest in your fist.

- Next, open your hand with the treat, and show him the treat. Close your hand if he tries to get the treat. Do this until he simply ignores the treat in the open hand, known as the decoy hand. When he ignores it, click and give your dog the treat from the other hand. Keep doing this until he ignores the treat in the open hand from the start of the exercise. When you have reached this point, add the command "leave it." Now, open the decoy hand, say "leave it" just once for each repetition, and when your dog does, click and treat him from the other hand.

- Now, put the treat on the floor and say, "leave it." Cover it with your hand if he tries to get it. When your dog looks away from the treat that is lying on the floor, click and treat your dog from the other hand. Continue issuing the command "leave it" until your dog no longer tries to get the treat that is on the floor.

-For the next exercise, put the treat on the floor and say, "leave it," and then stand up. Click and treat if he obeys. Now, walk your dog by the treat while he is on his leash and say, "leave it." If he goes for it, prevent this by restraining him with the leash. C/T him only when he ignores the treat. Increase the length of time between the leave it command and the C/T.

- Teaching your dog to leave it using a treat first, will allow you to work up to objects such as toys, animals, pills, spills, and even people. Once he gets the idea in his head that leave it means rewards for him, you both can eventually work towards more complex situations involving more difficult to resist items. Begin with a low value item such as a piece of kibble, then move to a piece of hard to resist meat, his favorite toy, another animal, or people.

- After your dog is successful at leaving alone the treat and other items, take the training outside into the yard, gradually adding people, toys, animals, and other hard to resist distractions. Next, head to the dog park, or any other place with even more distractions.

Remember to keep your puppy clear of dog parks until at least after his seventh week, preferably no sooner than his tenth week, and certainly only after his first round of vaccines. Some veterinarians and experts suggest even waiting until after the second round of vaccinations before your dog is exposed to other animals.

Continue practicing daily until your dog has this command down pat. This is another potential lifesaving command that you will use regularly during the life of your dog.

- At this point, you both can have some real fun. Try placing a dog biscuit on your pups paw, snout, or head and say, "leave it." Gradually increase the time that your pup must leave the biscuit in place. Try this when he is in the sitting and other down positions. Have some fun and be sure to reward your dog the biscuit after he leaves it undisturbed. ~ Enjoy!

- Gradually phase out clicking and treating your dog every time that on command he obeys "leave it." As with prior commands, begin gradually reducing treating by one out of two times, one out three times, then one out of four, five, six, and finally none. Remember not to decrease too quickly or it will undermine your training. Keenly observe your dog's abilities and pace at all times. The goal is that your dog will obey all the commands without a reward, eventually with only a vocal or physical cue.

"Down"

Teaching your Aire to lie down not only helps to keep him in one spot, but also offers a calming timeout, in addition, it is a useful intervention to curtail, or even prevent barking. When paired with the stay command, you can keep your dog comfortably in one place for long periods. Down not only protects your dog in potentially hazardous situations, but it also provides you with peace of mind that your dog will remain in the place where you commanded him to stay. This is yet another essential command that you will utilize daily, throughout the lifetime of your dog.

Basics

- Begin training in a quiet place with few distractions, and bring plenty of treats. Wait for your dog to lie down of his own will, and then *click and treat* while he is in the lying down position. Toss a treat to get him up again. Repeat this until he begins to lie down immediately after he gets the treat. His compliance means that he is starting to understand that good things come to him when he lies down, so in anticipation of this, he lays right back down.

- Now, augment the training with the addition of the verbal command of "down." As soon as your dog starts to lie down, say "down," and *click and treat*. From here on, only *click and treat* your dog when he lies down after your command.

- Next, practice this in a variety of areas and in situations of various distraction. Begin the practice indoors, then take it outside into your yard, and then wander into the neighborhood, and beyond. Remain patient in the more distracting locations. Situations to command your dog to lie down could be times when there are strangers present, when there is food nearby, or when the stereo or television is on. Anytime you are outdoors barbequing, having a party, in the park, or during your walks together are also excellent opportunities to practice this command. Maintain diligence with this training, and attempt to find situations of increasing levels of distraction where you might need to use the command "down." Remember that you are looking for consistent compliance.

The power and importance of the command "down" will prove to be one of the most useful of all to train and maintain during the life of your dog. After your success with the training of "down," you can then move to the combination command of "down-stay," which should be trained in order to keep your dog in place until you release him. Imagine the ease and joy when your pooch accompanies you to the local café, and he lays quietly, as well as *obediently*, at your feet while you drink your morning coffee, or when you eat your meal. Having an obedient companion is a very attractive and respected attribute of any responsible dog owner.

It is important to monitor and track your partner's progress by taking notes during his training, especially as you increase the distractions, highlighting where and when he needs more work, or attention.

- Gradually phase out clicking and treating your dog every time that he obeys the "down" command. Reduce the treats to one time out of two compliances, followed by one out of three, then one out of four, five, six, and finally stop altogether. Do not decrease the treats too rapidly and be sure to observe closely, your dog's abilities and pace. The goal of the training is to have your dog obey *all* commands with only a vocal or physical cue, *without a reward*.

PROBLEMS SOLVED

- If your dog will not comply with the down command, you need to return the training to a low distraction area, such as a bathroom. Unless your dog likes decorative bath soaps or vanity mirrors, and he may, there is not much to distract him in the bathroom. Continue the training there.

- If your dog does lie down, but pops right back up, be sure that you are only treating him when in the lying down position. In this way, your dog will sooner understand the correlation between the command, action, and the subsequent treat.

"Stay"

Stay is perhaps a command that you have looked forward to teaching, after all, it is up there on top of the list, as one of the most useful and used *essential* commands. This command can be paired with *sit* and *down*. With these combination commands under your belt, daily life with your companion will be made easier. Teaching your dog restraint has practical uses, as well. By reinforcing the wanted behavior of remaining in place, your dog will not end up in potentially dangerous situations, such as running out the door and into the street. This command also limits the possibility of your dog putting you in embarrassing or inconvenient situations, such as jumping up on people, or chasing the neighbor's pet kangaroo. Furthermore, it is a valuable command that teaches compliance, which facilitates better control of your dog. Stay not only teaches your dog patience, but also reinforces his understanding of who is in charge of the decision-making. After you have taught your dog *sit* and *down*, the stay command should be next on your training agenda, as they make for useful pairings.

- To begin with, find yourselves a quiet low distraction place, and bring plenty of treats. Give the sit command, and after he obeys, wait two-seconds before you *click and treat*. Continue practicing while gradually extending the duration of time between his compliance and his receiving the click and treat, thus reinforcing the length of time he is in the sit position. Work up to 10-15 seconds of sitting before clicking and treating.

- Next, you can begin to issue the combination sit-stay command, and this time you can add a hand signal to the mix. While you issue the command, his signal can simply be your flat hand directed towards his fuzzy little face, at about 12 inches/30 centimeters. You can also choose a unique hand signal of your own to use in conjunction with sit-stay, being careful to avoid the use of the middle finger, as not to offend the neighbors or passersby. Continue practicing while increasing the time he is in the sit position. Gradually increase the sit-stay time to one minute before you C/T.

- If your dog gets up during this training, it means you are moving too quickly. Try again with a shorter stay time goal, and then slowly increase the time your dog is to remain completely still. Continue practicing until your dog will stay for longer intervals. A good way to keep track of your dog's progress through each training session is by starting a training log. This is helpful for many reasons, including monitoring his compliance, goals, outcomes, as well as wanted and unwanted behaviors.

- **Now, it is time to test your progress.**

Now, say "sit-stay," and take one big step away from your dog, then C/T him for his obedience. Keep practicing this until you can take two big steps in any direction, away from your dog without him moving. It is essential that you return to treat your dog at the exact spot in which he stayed in place. Refrain from treating him if he rises, or if he comes to you.

Keep progressing with this exercise until you can take several steps away, eventually moving completely out of sight of your dog, while he stays stationary. Work towards the goal of him staying motionless for two full minutes while you are in his sight, followed by an additional two minutes that you remain out of his sight. By gradually increasing the stay-time interval during this training, you reinforce the stay-response behavior to the point that your dog will stay put *no matter what is going on.* Often dogs will simply lie down after a number of minutes in the stay position. Usually, after about five minutes my dog just lies down until I release him.

- Lastly, begin increasing the distractions, while practicing all that has been trained up to this point. As previously instructed, begin the practice indoors, and then take it outside into the yard, and then move away from the familiarity of your house and neighborhood. For obvious reasons, be patient in the more distracting locations. It is important to maintain a practice routine of at least five minutes per day, particularly in places with increasing distraction. During your training sessions, continue to add other people, animals, all in a variety of noisy and increasingly distracting environments. The desired outcome of this training is to have a dog that remains in place in any situation you both may encounter during your time together.

Now, repeat the above steps chronologically using the command "*down*."

- Gradually phase out clicking and treating your dog every time that on command he obeys a command. As previously instructed, phase out treating by reducing it gradually, first by treating one out of two times, then once out three times, followed by once out of four, five, six, and then finally refrain all together. Be sure not decrease the treats too quickly. Observe and take notes of your dog's abilities and pace. The goal is to have a dog that will obey all the commands without reward, and only by a vocal, or physical cue.

When finished with this section you should have the commands "sit-stay" and "down-stay" being obeyed. Take care not to train both commands in the same training sessions.

HELPFUL HINTS

- *Always* reward your dog in the location where he has remained in place. It is important to refrain from releasing him with a C/T while using the *come* command. This will invariably confuse the outcome of the training, and diminish the importance of the come command. Keep it clear and simple.

- Note when your dog decides not to participate. It could be that the training is getting too difficult, too quickly. Put variation in the stay-time, as well as in the location, when giving commands to your dog. Give the little fella a chance to learn at his own pace.

- Practice the command of *stay,* particularly before he meets a new person. Practice this also before he follows you out the door, or into the car, or in the course of feeding, *before* you put down his food bowl.

- If you encounter any difficulties, back up a step, or calmly resume later. Be aware that each dog has his own pace of learning, so your ongoing patience is crucial. It is best to simply laugh, smile, and roll with your dog's own natural abilities while enjoying the process of teaching and learning together. After all, this is all quality time spent while hanging out with your new best friend.

Leash Training

Training your Aire to the leash will probably be one of the hardest things you will do. However, in the end, it is very rewarding and can serve to strengthen the trust and bond between you and your dog. A leash, or lead, is simply the rope that tethers you to your companion. Though a strong, good quality and adjustable leash is key, a feature of greater significance is the collar, or harness. There is a variety of collars to choose from, and it is up to you to do some research to determine which one is best fit for your dog. Head collars and front attachment harnesses are a couple of choices. Make sure it is a good fit and that your dog is comfortable wearing it.

For the sake of your dog's self-esteem, please select one that is stylish and in current fashion. Remember, you don't want the other dogs to stare or tease. On this topic, be sure to keep your eyes peeled for my next book, entitled- *"Doggy Vanity; Styles & Fashion for the Narcissistic Modern Canine."*

Keep in mind some general guidelines suggested when choosing a collar. If you are small and your dog is large, or if your dog tends to be aggressive or powerful, you will need to exert the greatest control, so the sensible choice should be a head collar. Front attachment collars are an excellent choice for any dog or activity. Head and frontal attached collars should be used with leashes with a length of six feet (1.82 meters), or less. The reason for maintaining a shorter leash is that a longer lead length could allow your dog, if he bolts, to gain enough speed to injure himself when the lead runs out and becomes suddenly taut.

The main goal here is to get your dog to walk beside you without pulling against the leash. An effective method during training is simply to stop moving forward when your dog pulls on the lead, turn and walk the opposite direction. Then, when he obediently walks beside you, reward with treats, praise and affection to reinforce the wanted behavior. The following steps will help you train your dog to have excellent leash manners. Remember, *loose leash walking is the goal!*

Before moving forward to the next instructional step, please make sure that your dog consistently performs the target action of the training step that you are teaching. His consistent compliance is necessary for the success of this training so do not be inclined to hurry or rush this training.

Walking With You Is A Treat (The beginning)

Start by donning your dog with a standard harness fastened with a non-retractable leash that is about ten to twenty feet (3-6 meters) in length. Before starting the training session, remember to load up your pouch or pockets with top-notch treats and head out to the back yard or another familiar, quiet, low distraction outdoor spot. It is best if there are no other animals or people present during this initial phase.

First, decide whether you want your dog to walk along on your left or right side. It is at this side that you will treat your dog, and when you do, treat at your thigh level. Eventually, your dog will automatically come to that side because that is where the goodies can be found. Later, you can train your dog to walk on either side of you, but for now, stick with one side. In the future, training for both sides allows you the flexibility to maneuver your dog anywhere, whether out of harm's way, or for a more practical application, like easily walking on either side of the street.

- Place a harness or collar on your dog and attach the leash. Begin the training by randomly walking about the yard. When your dog decides to walk along with you, *click and treat* on the chosen side, at the level of your thigh. To "walk along with you" specifically refers to an action where your dog willingly joins you when you move along, in full compliance, and in a manner without applying any resistance to the lead. If he continues to walk on the correct side, and calmly with you, give him a *click and treat* with every step, or two, that you take together, thus reinforcing the desired behavior. Keep practicing this until your dog remains by your side, more often than not.

At this time, do not worry about over-treating your trainee; you will eventually reduce the frequency of delivery, eventually phasing out treats completely upon his successful mastering of this skill. If you are concerned with your companion's waistline, or girlish figure, you can deduct the training treats from the next meal.

- Repeat ambling around the yard with your pal in-tow, but this time walk at a faster pace than your prior session together. As before, when your dog decides to walk with you, give him a *click and treat* at thigh level of the chosen side. Keep practicing this until your dog consistently remains by your side, at this new pace. This leash training should occur over multiple sessions and days.

There is no need to rush any aspects of training. Remember to be patient with all training exercises, and proceed at a pace dictated by your dog's energy level, and his willingness to participate.

Eyes on the THIGHS (Second act)

Keeping your dog focused on the training at hand. Teaching him that you are in control of the leash is crucial.

This time, start walking around the yard and wait for a moment when your dog lags behind, or gets distracted by something else. At this time say, "let's go" to him, followed by a non-violent slap to your thigh to get his attention. Make sure you use a cheerful voice when issuing this command, and refrain from any harsh tactics that will intimidate your pooch, which can certainly undermine any training. When he pays attention to you, simply walk away. By doing this, it isolates the cue connected to this specific behavior, thus moving closer to your dog's grasp of the command.

- If your dog catches up with you *before* there is tension on the leash, *click and treat* him from the level of your thigh on the chosen side. *Click and treat* him again after he takes a couple of steps with you, and then continue to reinforce this with a C/T for the next few steps while he continues walking beside you. Remember, the outcome of this training is *loose leash walking*.

If your dog catches up *after* the leash has become taut, *do not treat him*. Begin again by saying, "let's go," then treat him after he takes a couple of steps with you. Only reinforce with C/T when he is compliant.

- If he does not come when you say, "let's go," continue moving until there is tension on the lead. At this point, stop walking and apply firm, but gentle pressure to the leash. When he begins to come toward you, praise him as he proceeds. When he gets to you, *do not treat him*, instead say, "let's go," and begin walking again. Click and treat your dog if he stays with you, and continue to C/T your dog for every step or two that he stays with you.

Keep practicing this step until he remains at your side while you both walk around the yard. If he moves away from you, redirect him with pressure to the lead and command cue of "let's go," followed up with a C/T when he returns to the appropriate position of walking obediently in tandem with you.

Do not proceed forward to subsequent steps of the training until your dog is consistently walking beside you with a loose leash, and is appropriately responding to the "let's go" command. It can sometimes take many days and sessions for your dog to develop this skill, so it is important for you to remain patient and diligent during this time. The outcome of this training is well worth your time and effort.

Oh! The things to smell and pee on (Third act)

Just like you, your dog is going to want to sniff things and go potty. During these times, you should be in control. While your dog is on the leash, and when he is in anticipation of his regular treating, or at about each five minute interval, say something like, "go sniff," "go play," "free time," or some other verbal cue that you feel comfortable saying, followed by some self-directed free time on the leash.

Keep in mind that this is a form of reward, but if he pulls on the leash, you will need to redirect with a "let's go" cue, followed by your walking in the opposite direction, quickly ending his free time. If your dog remains compliant, and does not pull on the leash before the allotted free time has elapsed, you are still the one that needs to direct the conclusion of free leash time, by saying, "let's go," coupled with your walking in the opposite direction.

Where's is my human? (Fourth act)

Using steps one through three, continue practicing leash walking in the yard. During the course of the training session, gradually shorten the lead until 6-foot (1.8meter) length remains. Now, change the direction and speed of your movements, being sure to *click and treat* your dog every time he is able to stay coordinated with the changes you have implemented.

As loose leashed walking becomes routine and second nature for your companion, you can start phasing out the click and treats. Reserve the C/T for situations involving new or difficult training points, such as keeping up with direction changes, or ignoring potential distractions.

Out in the Streets (Fifth act)

Now, it is time to take your dog out of the yard and onto the sidewalk for his daily walk. You will use the same techniques you used in your yard, only now you have to deal with more distractions.

Thank YOU! with a very Special, Free Gift!

Hi, it's me 'Paul' (Author, and 'new friend' I hope.)

Below is a picture of me during a family trip to Thailand. If you have never been, make plans to go, it is beautiful. My kids and I sure missed our dogs and we couldn't wait to get home and hug them. I mean WOW! What an impact our dogs have in our everyday love, family bonding, and happiness.

The reason we share this powerful bond is the information inside the unique Jump Start Guide that includes effective ways to understand, care and communicate with my dogs at a much higher level. The benefits and rewards of owning a dog are too many to mention here. ☺ I described my own personal favorites above ☺

Thank you for trusting me to guide you so that you experience the same happiness and peace of mind my family enjoys with our dogs. Now you too can experience that same joy! Download it today!

Please Accept my **Free Thank You Gift** !
the
"New Dog Training Jump Start Guide"

and

DOWNLOAD
Your Free Gift Copy - Below -Today!

"The lasting benefits you TOO can experience, will go WAY beyond the professional knowledge you will learn!"

Thanks Again!
~Paul

"Click it" to:

DOWNLOAD it HERE!

Or You Can Type This Address In Your Browser:
www.newdogtimes.com/jump-start-guide/

Distractions can come in all forms, including other dogs, friendly strangers, traffic, alarming noises, sausage vendors, feral chickens, taunting cats and a host of other potential interruptions and disturbances. It is during these times that you might want to consider alternate gear, such as a front attachment harness, or a halter collar, which fits over the head offering ultimate control over your companion. Arm yourself with your dog's favorite treats, apply the utmost patience, and go about your walk together in a deliberate and calm manner. Remember to utilize the "let's go," command cue when he pulls against his leash, or forgets that you exist. In this new setting, be sure to treat him when he walks beside you and then supersize the portions if your dog is obedient and does not pull on the lead during a stressful moment, or in an excitable situation. Lastly, do not forget to reward with periodic breaks for sniffing and exploring.

Stop and Go exercise (Sixth act)

Attach a 6-foot lead to the collar. With a firm hold on the leash, toss a treat or toy at about twenty feet (6 meters) ahead of you and your dog, then start walking toward it. If your dog pulls the leash and tries to get at the treat, use the "let's go" command and walk in the opposite direction of the treat. If he stays beside you without struggle while you walk toward the treat, allow him have it as a reward.

Practice this several times until your dog no longer pulls toward the treat and stays at your side, waiting for you to make the first move. The other underlying goal is that your dog should always look to you for direction and follow your lead before taking an action such as running after the toy while he is still leashed.

Switching Sides (Seventh Act)

After your dog is completely trained to the specific side chosen, and with a few months of successful loose leash walking practice under your belt, then you can begin the training again, targeting the opposing side that the two of you have previously trained towards. There is no need rush, so proceed with the training of the opposite side when you know the time is right, and you are both comfortable with changing it up a bit. As previously mentioned, a dog that is able to walk loose leashed, on either side of you is the desired, target outcome of this training. This skill is essential for navigating your dog, with ease and safety, in the outside world.

TROUBLE SHOOTING

- If your dog happens to cross in front of you during your time together, he may be distracted, so it is important to make your presence known to him with a gentle leash tug, or an appropriate command.

- If your dog is lagging behind you, he might be frightened or not feeling well, instead of pulling your dog along, give him a lot of support and encouragement. If the lagging is due to normal behavioral distractions, such as scent sniffing or frequent territorial marking, keep walking along. In this case, it is appropriate to pull gently on the leash to encourage his attention to the task at hand.

- The reinforcement of wanted behaviors necessitates you delivering numerous rewards when your dog walks beside you, or properly executes what it is you are training at that time. During your time together, pay close attention to your dog's moods, patterns and behaviors. You want to pay close attention to these things so that you can anticipate his responses, modify your training sessions, or simply adapt whatever it is you are doing to assure that his needs are being met, and you are both on the same page. Being conscious of your dog's needs will assist in maintaining a healthy, respectful bond between the two of you. Make an effort to use playful tones in your voice, with a frequent "good dog," followed by some vigorous petting, or some spirited play. Try to be aware of when your dog is beginning to tire, and attempt always to end a training session on a high note, with plenty of treats, play, and praise.

Heel

You will find this command indispensable when you are out and about, or perhaps when you encounter a potentially dangerous situation. There will be times where you will need to issue a firm command in order to maintain control of your dog in order to keep the both of you out of harms-way. *Heel* is that command.

During your time together exploring the outside world, things such as another aggressive dog, the busy traffic, a construction site, a teasing cat, or that irresistible squirrel may warrant keeping your dog close to you. If trained to the heel command, your dog will be an indispensable asset in helping to avert possible hazardous circumstances. The heel command is a clear instruction, trained to assure that your dog remains close beside you, *until you say otherwise*.

- Begin this training inside of your back yard, or in another low distraction area. First, place a treat in your fist on the side you've decided to train. Let him sniff your fist, then say "heel," followed by a few steps forward, leading him along with the fisted treat at thigh level. Click and treat him as he follows your fist with his nose. The fist is to keep your dog close to you. Practice for a few sessions.

- Next, begin the training as before, but now with an empty fist. With your fist held out in front of you, give the "heel" command, and then encourage your dog follow by your side. When he follows your fist for a couple of steps, *click and treat* him. For each subsequent session, repeat this practice a half dozen times, or more.

- Continue to practice heel while you are moving around, but now begin to increase the length of time *before* you treat your dog. Introduce a new direction in your walking pattern, or perhaps use a serpentine-like maneuver, snaking your way around the yard. You will want to continuously, but progressively challenge him in order to advance his skills, and to bolster his adaptability in various situations.

During all future outings together, this closed-empty-fist will now serve as your non-verbal, physical hand cue instructing your dog to remain in the heel position. From here on out, remember to display your closed-empty-fist at your side when you issue your heel command.

- Now, move the training sessions outside of the security of your yard. The next level of teaching should augment his learning by exposing him to various locations with increasingly more distractions. The implementation of this new variation in training is done to challenge, as well as to enhance your walking companion's adaptability to a variety of situations and stimulus.

Continue to repeat the *heel* command each time you take your dog out on the leash. Keeping his skills fresh with routine practice will ease your mind when out exploring new terrain together. Knowing that your dog will be obedient, and will comply with all of your commands, instructions and cues will be satisfying; in addition, it will keep you both safe and sane.

Out in the crazy, nutty world of ours there are plenty of instances when you will use this command to avoid unnecessary confrontations or circumstances with potentially dangerous outcomes.

If by chance you choose to use a different verbal cue other than the commonly used *heel* command, pick a word that is unique, and easy to say, and does not have a common use in everyday language. This way you avoid the possibility for confusion and misunderstanding."

"Go"

"Go" is a great cue to get your Airedale into his crate or onto his mat or rug, and later his *stuffed goose down micro-fiber plush bed*. This is a very handy command to send your dog to a specific location and keep him there while you tend to your business. Before teaching, "go," your dog should already be performing to the commands, *down*, *stay*, and of course responding to his or her *name*.

While training the following steps, do not proceed to the next step until your dog is regularly performing the current step.

- Find a quiet low distraction location to place a towel or mat on the floor and grab your treats. Put a treat in your hand and use it to lure your dog onto the towel while saying, "Go." When all four paws are on the towel, *click and treat* your dog. Do this about ten to fifteen times.

- Start the same way as above, say "go," but this time have an empty hand, act as though you have a treat in your fist while you are luring your dog onto the mat. When all fours are on the mat *click and treat* your dog. Do this ten to fifteen times.

- Keep practicing with an empty hand and eventually turning the empty hand into a pointed index finger. Point your finger towards the mat. If your dog does not understand, walk him to the mat then click and treat. Do this about ten to fifteen times.

- Now, cue with "go" *while pointing* to the towel, but do not walk to the towel with him. If your dog will not go to the towel when you point and say the command, then keep practicing the step above before trying this step again. Now proceed practicing the command "go" while using the pointed finger and when your dog has all four paws on the mat, click, and then walk over and treat him while he is on the mat. Do this about ten to fifteen times.

- Now, grab your towel and try this on different surfaces and other places, such as grass, tile, patio, carpet, and in different rooms. Continue to practice this in more and more distracting situations and don't forget your towel or mat. Take the mat outdoors, to your friends and families houses, hotel rooms, the cabin, and any other place that you have your trusted companion with you.

One Step Beyond – "Relax"

In accordance with "go" This is an extra command you can teach. This is a single word command that encapsulates the command words go, down, and stay all into one word. The purpose is to teach your dog to go to a mat and lie on it until he is released. This is for when you need your dog out from under foot for extended lengths of time, such as when you are throwing a party. Pair it with "down and stay" so your dog will go the mat, lie down, and plan on staying put for an extended period of time. You can substitute your own command, such as "settle," "rest," or "chill," but once you choose a command stick with it and remain consistent.

This command can be used anywhere that you go, letting your dog know that he will be relaxing for a long period and to assume his relaxed posture. You can train this command when your pup is young and it will benefit you and him throughout your life together.

- Place your mat, rug, or what you plan using for your dog to lie.

- Give the "go" command and C/T your dog when he has all four paws on the mat. While your dog is on the mat, issue the command "down stay," then go to him and C/T while your dog is still on the mat.

- Now, give the "relax" command and repeat the above exercise with this "relax" command. Say, "relax," "go" and C/T your dog when he has all four paws on the mat. While your dog is on the mat, issue the command "down stay," and C/T while your dog is still on the mat. When your dog understands the "relax" command it will incorporate go, down, and stay.

Practice 7-10 times per session until your dog is easily going to his mat, lying down, and staying in that position until you release him.

- Next, give only the "relax" command and wait for your dog to go to the mat and lie down *before* you *click and treat* your dog. Do not use any other cues at this time. Continue practicing over multiple sessions, 7-10 repetitions per session, so that your dog is easily following your one word instruction of "relax."

- Now begin making it more difficult; vary the distance, add distractions, and increase the times in the relax mode. This is a wonderful command for keeping your dog out of your way for lengthy durations. You will love it when this command is flawlessly followed.

HELPFUL HINT

-While you are increasing the time that your dog maintains his relaxed position, click and treat every 5-10 seconds.

- You can also shape this command so that your dog assumes a more relaxed posture than when you issue "down stay." When your dog realizes that the "relax" command encompasses the super relaxed posture that he would normally use under relaxed conditions, he will understand that he will most likely be staying put for a lengthy period and your dog might as well get very comfortable.

Another obedience command that can and should be taught is the release command. Do not forget to teach a release command word to release your dog from any previous command. Release is command #14 in my 49 ½ Dog Tricks book that will soon, or is already for purchase. *Release* is easier to train if your dog already *sits* and *stays* on command.

This command informs your dog that they are free to move from whichever previous command you had issued and your dog complied, such as *sit, down,* and when combined with *stay*. When released your dog should rise from the position but remain in place. This is an obedience command that can keep your dog safe and you from worrying about your dog bolting off or moving at the wrong time during a potentially dangerous situation. You can choose any command, such as "move," or "break." As a reminder, one or two syllable words work best when teaching dogs commands.

Jumping is a NO-NO

Your dog loves you and wants as much attention from you as possible. The reality is that you are the world to your dog. Often when your dog is sitting quietly, he is easily forgotten. When he is walking beside you, you are probably thinking about other things, such as work, dinner, the car, chores you need to accomplish, or anything but your loyal companion walking next to you. Sometimes your dog receives your full attention only when he jumps up on you. When your dog jumps up on you, then you look at him, physically react in astonishment, maybe shout at him, and gently push him down until he is down on the floor. Then, you ignore him again, and make a mental note to teach your dog not to jump up onto you. What do you expect? He wants your attention. Teaching your dog not to jump is essentially teaching him that attention will come only if he has all four paws planted firmly on the ground.

It is important not to punish your dog when teaching him not to jump up on you and others. Do not shout "no!" or "bad!" Do not knee your dog or push him down. The best way to handle the jumping is to turn your back and ignore your dog. Remember, since he loves you very much, your dog or puppy may take any physical contact from you as a positive sign. You do not want to send mixed signals; instead, you want to practice complete ignoring that consists of no looking or audio. If you do use a vocal command, do not say, "off," instead use "sit," which your dog has probably already learned. Try not to use a command, and instead proceed with ignoring.

For jumping practice, it would be ideal if you could gather a group of people together who will participate in helping you train your dog that jumping is a no-no. You want to train your dog to understand that he will only get attention if he is on the ground. If groups of people are not available, then teach him to remain grounded using his family. When your dog encounters other people, use a strong "sit stay" command to keep all four paws planted firmly on the ground. I covered "sit stay" above, and now you understand how useful and versatile this command can be.

No Jumping On the Family

This is the easiest part, because the family and frequent visitors have more chances to help your dog or puppy to learn. When you come in from outside and your dog starts jumping up, say, "oops!" or "whoa," and immediately leave through the same door. Wait a few seconds after leaving and then do it again. When your dog finally stops jumping upon you as you enter, give him a lot of attention. Ask the rest of the family to follow the same protocol when they come into the house. If you find that he is jumping up at other times as well, like when you sing karaoke, walking down the hallway, or are cooking at the barbeque, just ignore your dog by turning your back and put energy into giving him attention when he is sitting.

No Jumping on Others

Prevention is of utmost importance and the primary focus in this exercise, especially with larger dogs. You can prevent your dog from jumping by using a leash, a tieback, crate, or gate. Until you have had enough practice and your dog knows what you want him to do, you really should use one of these methods to prevent your dog from hurting someone or getting an inadvertent petting reward for jumping. To train, you will need to go out and solicit some dog training volunteers and infrequent visitors to help.

- Make what is called a *tieback*, which is a leash attached to something sturdy, within sight of the doorway but not blocking the entrance keeping your dog a couple of feet or about a meter away from the doorway. Keep this there for a few months during the training period until your dog is not accosting you or visitors. When the guest arrives, hook your dog to the secure leash and then let the guest in.

Guests Who Want to Help Train Your Dog (Thank you in advance)

All of these training sessions may take many sessions to complete, so remain patient and diligent in training and prevention until your dog complies with not jumping on people.

- Begin at home, and when a guest comes in through the door, and the dog jumps up, they are to say "oops" or "whoa," and leave immediately. Practice this with at least five or six different visitors, each making multiple entrances during the same visit. If your helpers are jumped, have them completely ignore your dog by not making any eye contact, physical or vocal actions other than the initial vocal word towards your dog, then have them turn their backs and immediately leave.

- When you go out onto the streets, have your dog leashed. Next, have your guest helper approach your dog. If he strains against the leash or jumps have the guest turn their back and walk away. When your dog calms himself and sits, have the guest approach again. Repeat this until the guest can approach, pet and give attention to your dog without your dog jumping up. Have the volunteer repeat this at least five to seven times. Remember to go slowly and let your dog have breaks. Keep the sessions in the 5-7 minute range. For some dogs, this type of training can get frustrating. Eventually, your dog will understand that his jumping equals being ignored.

- Use the tie-back that you have placed near the door. Once your dog is calm, the visitor can greet your dog if they wish. If the guest does not wish to greet your dog, give your dog a treat to calm his behavior. If he barks, send your dog to his crate or the gated time out area. The goal is that you always greet your guests first, *not your dog*. Afterward, your guests have the option to greet or not greet, instead of your dog always rushing in to greet every guest. If he is able to greet guests calmly while tied back, then he may be released. At first hold the leash to see how your dog reacts, then if he is calm release him.

A Caveat to These Two Methods

1) For those who are not volunteers to help teach your dog and are at your home visiting, there is another method. Keep treats by the door, and as you walk in throw them seven to nine feet (2.1 - 2.7 meters) away from you. Continue doing this until your dog begins to anticipate this. Once your dog is anticipating treats every time someone comes through the door it will keep him from accosting you or visitors that walk through the doorway. After your dog eats his treat and he has calmed down a bit, ask him to sit, and then give him some good attention.

2) Teach your dog that a hand signal such as grabbing your left shoulder means the same as the command "sit." By combining the word "sit" with a hand on your left shoulder, he will learn this. If you want to use another physical cue, you can substitute your own gesture here, such as holding your left wrist or ear.

Ask the guests that have volunteered to help train your dog to place their right hand on their left shoulders and wait until your dog *sits* before they pet him or give any attention. Training people that meet your dog will help both you and your dog in preventing unwanted excitement and jumping up. Having your dog sit before he can let loose with jumps is proactive jumping prevention.

Barking

Any dog owner knows that dogs bark for many reasons, most commonly, for attention. Your Aire may bark for play, attention, or because it is close to feeding time and he wants you to feed him. Dogs also bark to warn intruders and us so we also need to understand why our dog is barking. Not all barking is bad. Some dogs are short duration barkers, and others can go on for hours, we do not want that and either do our neighbors.

Whatever the case, *don't do it*. Do not give your dog attention for barking. Do not send the signals that your dogs barking gets an immediate reaction from you, such as you coming to see why he is barking or moving towards him. As I mentioned in the opening paragraph, they do sometimes bark to warn us, so we shouldn't ignore all barking, we need to assess the barking situation before dismissing it as nonsense barking. When you know the cause is a negative behavior that needs correction, say, "leave it" and ignore him. While not looking at your dog go to the other side of the room, or into another room, you can even close the door behind you until your dog has calmed down. Make it clear to your barking dog that his barking does not result in any rewards or attention.

In everyday life, make sure you are initiating activities that your dog enjoys and always making them happen on *your* schedule. You are the alpha leader so regularly show your pup who is in charge. Also, make sure that he earns what he is provided. Have your pup *sit* before he gets the reward of going outside to play, a toy, his bowl of food, or loaded into the car to go tailgating (home team jersey not included).

Your dog may bark when seeing or hearing something interesting. Below are a few ways to deal with this issue.

Prevention when you are at your residence

- *Teach your dog the command "quiet."* When your dog barks, wave a piece of food in front of his nose at the same time you are saying, "quiet." When he stops barking to sniff, *click and treat* him right away. Do this about four or five times. Then the next time he barks, pretend you have a piece of food in your hand next to his nose and say, "quiet." Always *click and treat* him as soon as he *stops* barking. After issuing the "quiet" command, *click and treat* him again for every few seconds that he remains quiet. Eventually, as you make your way to five or ten seconds, gradually increase the time lapses between the command "quiet," and *clicking and treating*.

- *Prevent it.* Block the source of sound or sight so that your dog is unable to see or hear the catalyst that is sparking his barking. Use a fan, stereo, TV, curtains, blinds, or simply put him in a different area of the house to keep him away from the stimulus.

- When your pup hears or sees something that would usually make him bark and he *does not bark*, reward him with attention, play, or a treat. This is reinforcing and shaping good behaviors instead of negative behaviors.

The Time Out

- We use it on our children, and yes you can you can use a *time out* on your dog, but do not use it too often. When you give your dog a time out, you are taking your dog out of his social circle and giving your dog what is known as a negative punishment. This kind of punishment is powerful and can have side effects that you do not want. Your dog may begin to fear you when you walk towards him, especially if you have the irritated look on your face that he recognizes as the *time out face*. The *time out* should be used very sparingly. Focus on teaching your dog the behaviors that you prefer while preventing the bad behavior.

Choose a place where you want the time out spot to be. Make sure that this place is not the potty spot, the play area, or the *Saturday night square dancing spot*. Ideally it is a boring place that is somewhere that is not scary, not too comfortable, but safe. A gated pantry or the bathroom can work well. If your puppy does not mind his crate, you can use it. Secure a 2-foot piece of rope or a short leash to your puppy's collar. When your pup barks, use a calm voice and give the command, "time out," then take the rope and walk him firmly but gently to the time out spot. Leave him there for about 5 minutes, longer if necessary. When your dog is calm and not barking you can release him. You may need to do this two to a dozen times before he understands which behavior has put him into the time out place. Most dogs are social and love being around their humans, so this can have a strong impact.

Prevention when you are away from your residence

- Again, prevent barking by blocking the sounds or sights that are responsible for your dog or puppy going into barking mode. Use a fan, stereo, curtain, blinds, or keep him in another part of the house away from the stimulus.

- Use a Citronella Spray Collar. Only use this for when the barking has become intolerable. Do not use this when the barking is associated with fear or aggression. You will want to use this a few times when you are at home, so that your dog understands how it works.

Citronella collars work like this. The collar has a sensitive microphone, which senses when your dog is barking, when this happens it triggers a small release of citronella spray into the area above a dog's nose. It surprises the dog and disrupts barking by emitting a smell that dogs dislike.

Out walking

While you are out walking your dog, out of shear excitement or from being startled, he might bark at other dogs, people, cars, and critters. This can be a natural reaction or your dog may have sensitivities to certain tones, the goal is to try to limit the behavior and quickly cease the barking.

Here are some helpful tools to defuse that behavior.

- Teach your dog the *"watch me"* command. Begin this training in the house where there are fewer distractions. While you hold a treat to your nose, say your dog's name and "watch me." When your dog looks at the treat for at least one second give him a click and treat. Repeat this about 10-15 times. Then increase the time that your dog looks at you to 2-3 seconds, and repeat a dozen times.

- Then, repeat the process while pretending to have a treat on your nose. You will then want to incorporate this hand to your nose as your hand signal for *watch me*. *Click and treat* when your dog looks at you for at least one second, then increase to two or three seconds, and *click and treat* after each goal. Repeat this about 10-15 times.

- Increase the duration that your dog will continue to watch you while under the command. Continue practicing while increasing the length of time your dog will watch you. Click and treat as your progress. Try to keep your dog's attention for 5-10 seconds. Holding your dog's attention for this length of time usually results in the catalyst to move away from the area or for your dog to lose interest.

- Now, practice the "watch me" command while you are walking around inside the house. Then practice this again outside. When outside, practice near something he finds interesting. Practice in a situation that he would normally bark. Continue practicing in different situations and around other catalysts that you know will set your dog off barking.

This is a great way to steer attention towards you and away from your dog's barking catalysts.

Other Solutions

- When you notice something that normally makes your dog bark and he has not begun to bark, use the "quiet" command. For example, your dog regularly barks at the local skateboarder. When the trigger that provokes your dog's barking, the skateboarder comes zooming by, use the command "quiet," and *click and treat*. Click and treat your dog for every few seconds that he remains quiet. Teach your dog that his barking trigger gets him a "quiet" command. Your dog will begin to associate the skateboarder with treats and gradually it will diminish his barking outbursts at the skateboarder.

- If he frequently barks while a car is passing by, put a treat by his nose, and then bring it to your nose. When he looks at you, *click and treat* him. Repeat this until he voluntarily looks at you when a car goes by and does not bark, continuing to *treat* him appropriately.

- You can also reward your dog for calm behavior. When you see something or encounter something that he would normally bark at and he does not, *click and treat* your dog. Instead of treats, sometimes offer praise and affection

- If you are out walking and your dog has not yet learned the *quiet* cue, or is not responding to it, turn around and walk away from whatever is causing your dog to bark. When he calms down, offer a reward.

- As a last resort use the citronella spray collar if your dogs barking cannot be controlled using the techniques that you have learned. Use this only when the barking is *not* associated with fear or aggression.

Your dog is Afraid, Aggressive, Lonely, Territorial, or Hung-over

Your dog may have outbursts when he feels territorial, aggressive, lonely, or afraid. All of these negative behaviors can be helped with proper and early socialization, but occasionally they surface. Many times rescue dogs might have not been properly socialized and bring their negative behaviors into your home. Be patient while you are teaching your new dog proper etiquette. If your dog is prone to territorialism, it can be a challenge to limit his barking.

- This is not a permanent solution, but is a helpful solution while you are teaching your dog proper barking etiquette. To allow your dog a chance to find his center, relax his mind and body, do this for about seven to ten days before beginning to train against barking. As a temporary solution, you should first try to prevent outbursts by crating, gating, blocking windows, using fans or music to hide sounds, and avoid taking your dog places that can cause these barking outbursts.

SOME TIPS

- Always, remain calm, because a relaxed and composed alpha achieves great training outcomes. A confident, calm, cool, and collected attitude that states you are unquestionably in charge goes a long way in training.

- If training is too stressful or not going well, you may want to hire a professional positive trainer for private sessions. When interviewing, tell him or her that you are using a clicker and rewards based training system and are looking for a trainer that uses the same type or similar methods.

It is important to help your dog to modify his thinking about what tends to upset him. Teach him that what he was upset about before now predicts his favorite things. Here is how.

- When the trigger appears in the distance, *click and treat* your dog. Keep clicking and treating your dog as the two of you proceed closer to the negative stimulus.

- If he is territorially aggressive, teach him that the doorbell or a knock on the door means that is his cue to get into his crate and wait for treats. You can do this by ringing the doorbell and luring your dog to his crate and once he is inside the crate giving him treats.

- You can also lure your dog through his fears. If you are out walking and encounter one of his triggers, put a treat to his nose and lead him out and away from the trigger zone.

- Use the "watch me" command when you see him getting nervous or afraid. *Click and treat* him frequently for watching you.

- Reward *calm* behavior with praise, toys, play, or treats.

- *For the hangover, I recommend lots of sleep.*

Your dog is frustrated, bored or both

All dogs including your dog or puppy may become bored or frustrated. At these times, your dog may lose focus, not pay attention to you, and *spend time writing bad poetry in his journal*. Here are a few things that can help prevent this:

- Keep him busy and tire him out with chew toys, exercise, play, and training. These things are a cure for most negative behaviors. A tired dog is usually happy to relax and enjoy quiet time.

- He should have at least 30 minutes of aerobic exercise per day. In addition to the aerobic exercise, each day he should have an hour of chewing and about 15 minutes of training. Keep it interesting for him with a variety of activities. It is, after all, the spice of life.

- Use the command "quiet" or give your dog a time out.

- As a last resort, you can break out the citronella spray collar.

Excited to Play

- Like an actor in the wings, your puppy will get excited about play. Teach your dog that when he starts to bark, the play stops. Put a short leash on him and if he barks, use it to lead him out of play sessions. Put your dog in a time out or just stop playing with your dog. Reward him with more play when he calms down.

Armed with these many training tactics to curb and stop barking, you should be able to gradually reduce your dogs barking, and help him to understand that some things are not worth barking at all. Gradually you will be able to limit the clicking and treating, but it is always good practice to reward your dog for not barking and behaving in the manner you desire. Reward your dog with supersized treat servings for making the big breakthroughs.

Nipping & Biting

Friendly and feisty, little puppies nip for a few reasons; they are teething, playing or they want to get your attention. My Uncle Jimmy nips from a bottle, but that is a *completely different story*. If you have acquired yourself a nipper, not to worry, in time most puppies will grow out of this behavior on their own. Other dogs, such as those bred for herding, nip as a herding instinct. They use this behavior to round up their animal charges, other animals, family members, including those who are *human*.

While your dog is working through the nipping stage, you will want to avoid punishing or correcting your dog because this could eventually result in a strained relationship down the road. However, you will want to teach your puppy how delicate human skin is. Let your dog test it out and give him feedback. You can simply indicate your discomfort when he bites too hard, by using and exclamation, such as, *"yipe!"*, *"youch!"*, or *"Bowie!"* This in addition to a physical display of your pain by pulling back your hand, calf or ankle, will usually be enough for your dog to understand that it is not an acceptable behavior. After this action, it is important to cease offering any further attention towards your dog, because this offers the possibility that the added attention will reinforce the negative behavior. If you act increasingly more sensitive to the nips, he will begin to understand that we humans are very sensitive, and will quickly respond with a sudden vocal and physical display of discomfort.

This is a very easy behavior to modify because we know the motivation behind it. The puppy wants to play and chew, and who is to blame him for this? Remember, it is important to give your dog access to a variety of chew-toys, and when he nips, respond accordingly, then immediately walk away and ignore him. If he follows you, and nips at your heels, give your dog a time out. Afterward, when your dog is relaxed, calm and in a gentle disposition, stay and play with him. Use the utmost patience with your puppy during this time, and keep in mind that this behavior will eventually pass.

Herding dogs will not so easily be dissuaded, though. For these breeds, it is not always possible to curb this behavior entirely, but you can certainly limit or soften it, eventually making them understand that nipping humans is a *no-no*, and *very painful*. To address this more thoroughly, between the ages of four to five months herding dogs can be enrolled in behavioral classes. This will reinforce your training and boost what you are training at home.

Preventing the "Nippage"

- Always have a chew toy in your hand when you are playing with your puppy. This way he learns that the right thing is to bite and chew is the toy, and is *not your hands, or any other part of your body.*

- Get rid of your puppy's excess energy by exercising him *at least* an hour each day. As a result, he will have no energy remaining to nip.

- Make sure he is getting adequate rest and that he is not cranky from lack of sleep. Twelve hours per day is good for dogs, and it seems for teenagers as well.

- Always have lots of interesting chew toys available to help your puppy to cope during the teething process.

- Teach your kids not to run away screaming from nipping puppies. They should walk away quietly, or simply stay still. Children should never be left unsupervised when around dogs.

- Play with your puppy in his gated puppy area. This makes it easier to walk away if he will not stop biting or mouthing you. This quickly reinforces his understanding that hard bites end play sessions.

- As a last resort, when the other interventions and methods discussed above are not working, you should increase the frequency of your use of a tieback to hold your dog in place, within a gated or time out area. If your dog is out of control with nipping or biting, and you have not yet trained him that biting is an unacceptable behavior, you may have to use this method until he is fully trained. For example, you may want to use this when guests are over, or if you simply need a break. Always use a tieback while your dog is under supervision, and never leave him tied up alone. The tieback is a useful method and can be utilized as a tool of intervention when addressing other attention getting behaviors like jumping, barking, and the dreaded leg humping.

The best option during this time, early in his training, is to place him in a room with a baby gate in the doorway.

Instructing Around the "Nippage"

- Play with your dog and praise him for being gentle. When he nips say, *"yipe!"* mimicking the sound of an injured puppy, and then immediately walk away. After the nipping, wait one minute and then return to give him another chance at play, or simply remain in your presence *without nipping*. Practice this for two or three minutes, remembering to give everyone present or those who will have daily contact with him a chance to train him through play. It is crucial that puppies *do not receive any reward for nipping*. After an inappropriate bite or nip, all physical contact needs to be abruptly stopped, and quick and complete separation needs to take place so that your puppy receives a clear message.

- After your puppy begins to understand that bites hurt, and if he begins to give you a softer bite, *continue to act hurt, even if it doesn't*. In time, your dog will understand that only the slightest pressures by mouth are permissible during play sessions. Continue practicing this until your puppy is only using the softest of mouths, and placing limited tension upon your skin.

- Next, the goal is to decrease the frequency of mouthing. You can use the verbal cues of *quit* or *off* to signal that his mouth needs to release your appendage. Insist that the amount of time your puppy uses his mouth on you needs to decrease in duration, as well as the severity of pressure needs to decrease. If you need incentive, use kibble or liver to *reward after you command and he obeys.* Another reward for your puppy when releasing you from his mouth grasp is to give him a chew or chew-toy stuffed with food.

- The desired outcome of this training is for your puppy to understand that mouthing any human, if done at all, should be executed with the utmost care, and in such a manner, that without question the pressure *will not inflict pain or damage.*

- Continue the training using the verbal cue of *quit,* until *quit* becomes a well-understood command, and your dog consistently complies when it is used. Interject breaks every 20-30 seconds when playing and any type of mouthing is occurring. The calm moments will allow excitement to wane, and will help to reduce the chances of your dog excitably clamping down. Practice this frequently, and as a part of your regular training practice schedule. The result from successful training and knowing that your dog will release upon command will give you piece of mind.

- If you have children, or are worried about the potential for injury due to biting, you can continue training in a way that your dog knows that mouthing is *not permitted under any circumstance.* This level of training permits you from having to instruct a permissible mouthing pressure. This will result in a reduction of your anxiety whenever your dog is engaged in playing with your family or friends. This of course nearly eliminates the potential for biting accidents occurring.

Be vigilant when visitors are playing with your dog. Monitor the play, and be especially attentive to the quality of the interaction, being alert to understand that the session is not escalating into a rough and potentially forceful situation in which your dog might choose to use his mouth in an aggressive or harmful way. You will need to decide the rules of engagement, and it will be your responsibility that others understand these rules. To avoid harm or injury it will be necessary for you to instruct visitors and family prior to play.

Digging Help

Some dogs are going to dig no matter what you do to stop it. For these diggers, this behavior is bred into them, so remember that these dogs have an urge to do what they do. Whether this behavioral trait is for hunting or foraging, it is deeply imbedded inside their DNA and it is something that cannot be turned off easily, or at all. Remember that when you have a digger for a dog, they will tend to be excellent escape artists, so you will need to bury your perimeter fencing deep to keep them inside your yard or kennel.

Cold weather dogs such as Huskies, Malamutes, Chows, and other "Spitz" type dogs often dig a shallow hole in an area to lie down in, to either cool down, or warm up. These dogs usually dig in a selected and distinct area, such as in the shade of a tree or shrub.

Other natural diggers such as Terriers, and Dachshunds, are natural hunters and dig to bolt or hold prey at bay for their hunting companions. These breeds have been genetically bred for the specific purpose of digging into holes to chase rabbits, hare, badgers, weasels, and other burrowing animals. Scenthounds such as Beagles, Bassets, and Bloodhounds will dig under fences in pursuit of their quarry. This trait is not easily altered or trained away, but you can steer it into the direction of your choosing. To combat dog escapes you will need to bury your fencing or chicken wire deep into the ground. It is suggested that 18-24 inches, or 46-61cm into the soil below the bottom edge of your fencing is sufficient, but we all know that a determined dog may even go deeper, when in pursuit of quarry. Some dog owners will affix chicken wire at about 12 inches (30.5cm) up onto the fence, and then bury the rest down deep into the soil. Usually, when the digging dog reaches the wire, its efforts will be thwarted and it will stop digging.

Some dogs dig as an instinctive impulse to forage for food to supplement their diet. Because dogs are omnivorous, they will sometimes root out tubers, rhizomes, bulbs, or any other edible root vegetable that is buried in the soil. Even nuts buried by squirrels, newly sprouting grasses, the occasional rotting carcass or other attractive scents will be an irresistible aroma to their highly sensitive noses.

Other reasons dogs dig can be traced directly to boredom, lack of exercise, lack of mental and physical stimulation, or improperly or under-socialized dogs. Improperly socialized dogs can suffer from separation anxiety and other behavioral issues. Non-neutered dogs may dig an escape to chase a female in heat. Working breeds such as Border Collies, Australian Cattle Dogs, Shelties, and other working breeds can stir up all sorts of trouble if not kept busy. This trouble can include incessant digging.

It has been said that the smell of certain types of soil can also catch a dog's fancy. Fresh earth, moist earth, certain mulches, topsoil, and even sand are all lures for the digger. If you have a digger, you should fence off the areas where you are using these alluring types of soils. These kinds of soils are often used in newly potted plants or when establishing a flowerbed or garden. The smell of dirt can sometimes attract a dog that does not have the strong digging gene, but when he finds out how joyful digging can be, beware; you can be responsible for the creation of your own "Frankendigger."

Proper socialization, along with plenty of mental and physical exercises will help you in your fight against digging, but as we know, some diggers are going to dig no matter what the situation. Just in case your dog or puppy is an earnest excavator, here are some options to help you curb that urge.

The Digging Pit

A simple and fun solution is to dig a pit specifically for him or her to dig to their little heart's content. Select an appropriate location, and with a spade, turn over the soil a bit to loosen it up, mix in some sand to keep it loose as well as to improve drainage, then surround it with stones or bricks to make it obvious by sight that this is the designated spot.

To begin training your dog to dig inside the pit, you have to make it attractive and worth their while. First bury bones, chews, or a favorite toy, then coax your dog on over to the pit to dig up some treasures. Keep a watchful eye each time you bring your dog out, and do not leave him or her unsupervised during this training time. It is important to halt immediately any digging outside of the pit. When they dig inside of the designated pit, be sure to reward them with treats and praise. If they dig elsewhere, direct them back to the pit. Be sure to keep it full of the soil-sand mixture, and if necessary, littered with their favorite doggie bootie. If your dog is not taking to the pit idea, an option is to make the other areas where they are digging temporarily less desirable such as covering them with chicken wire, and then making the pit look highly tantalizingly, like a *doggie digging paradise*.

Buried Surprises

Two other options are leaving undesirable surprises in the unwanted holes your dog has begun to dig. A great deterrent is to place your dog's own *doodie* into the holes that he has dug, and when your dog returns to complete his job, he will not enjoy the gift you have left him, thus deterring him from further digging.

Another excellent deterrent is to place an air-filled balloon inside the hole and then cover it with soil. When your dog returns to his undertaking and then his little paws burst the balloon, the resulting loud "POP!" sound will startle, and as a result, your dog will reconsider the importance of his or her mission. After a few of these shocking noises, you should have a dog that thinks twice before digging up your bed of pansies.

Shake Can Method

This method requires a soda can or another container filled with rocks, bolts, or coins, remembering to place tape or apply the cap over the open end to keep the objects inside. Keep this "rattle" device nearby so that when you let your dog out into the yard you can take it with you to your clandestine hiding spot. While hidden out of sight, simply wait until our dog begins to dig. Immediately at the time of digging, take that can of coins and shake it vigorously, thereby startling your dog. Repeat the action each time your dog begins to dig, and after a few times your dog should refrain from further soil removal. Remember, the goal is to *startle* and to distract your dog at the time they initiate their digging, and not to terrorize your little friend.

Shake can instructions

1. Shake it quickly once or twice then stop. The idea is to make a sudden and disconcerting noise that is unexpected by your dog who is in the process of digging. If you continue shaking the can, it will become an ineffective technique.

2. Beware not to overuse this method. Remember your dog *can become desensitized* to the sound, and thus ignore the prompt.

3. Sometimes, it is important to supplement this method by using commands, such as "No" or "Stop."

4. Focus these techniques, targeting only the behavior (e.g. digging) that you are trying to eliminate.

5. Sometimes, a noise made by a can with coins inside may not work, but perhaps using a different container filled with nuts and bolts, or other items will. Examples are soda or coffee cans that are filled with coins, nuts, bolts, or other metal objects. You might have to experiment to get an effective and disruptive sound. If the noise you make sets off prolonged barking instead of a quick startled bark, then the sound is obviously not appropriate. If your dog does begin to bark after you make the noise, use the "quiet" command immediately after, and never forget to reward your dog when he or she stops the barking, thereby reinforcing the wanted behavior.

I hope that these methods will assist you in controlling or guiding your four-legged landscaper in your desired direction. Anyone that has had a digger for a dog knows it can be challenging. Just remember that tiring them out with exercise and games is often the easiest and most effective in curbing unwanted behaviors.

~ Paps

BASIC CARE

Basic Care for all dog breeds

Oral maintenance, clipping, and other grooming will depend upon you and your dog's activities. We all know our dogs love to roll and run through all sorts of possible ugly messes, and put obscene things into their mouths, then afterward run up to lick us. Below is a list of the basic grooming care your dog requires. Pick up a grooming book on your specific breed so that you know what and how often your dog needs particular services, extra care areas, and what you may need to have done by professionals.

Most basic care can easily be done at home by you, but if you are unsure or uncomfortable about something, get some tutelage and in no time you will be clipping, trimming, and brushing like a professional.

Coat Brushing - Daily brushing of your dog's coat can be done or at least a minimum of three to four times a week depending upon the condition of the coat. Some breeds blow their coat once or twice a year and daily brushing is recommended during this period. Many breeds do not require daily brushing but it is still healthy for the coat and skin.

Some Equipment: Longhaired dogs need pin brushes, short, medium, and some longhaired dogs need bristle brushes. Slicker brushes remove mats and dead hair. Rubber Curry Combs polish smooth coats. Some of the grooming tools available are clippers, stripping knives, rakes, and more.

Bathing - Regular but not frequent bathing is essential. Much depends upon your breed's coat. Natural coat oils are needed to keep your dog's coat and skin moisturized. Never bathe your dog too frequently. Depending upon what your dog has been into, a bath once month is adequate. For most breeds, bathing should be done at least once per month, with plenty of warm water and a gentle shampoo or soap made for dogs. Some breeds only require bathing when the odor can no longer be tolerated, so again, read up on your breeds needs.

Nail trimming – For optimal foot health, your dog's nails should be kept short. There are special clippers that are needed for nail trimming that are designed to avoid injury. You can start trimming when your dog is a puppy, and you should have no problems. However, if your dog still runs for the hills or squirms like an eel at trimming time, then your local groomer or veterinarian can do this procedure.

Ear cleaning – You should clean your dog's ears at least once a month depending upon your breed, but be sure to inspect them every few days for bugs such as mites and ticks. Also, look for any odd discharge, which can be an indication of infection, requiring a visit to the vet. Remember to clean the outer ear only, by using a damp cloth or a cotton swab doused with mineral oil.

Eye cleaning - Use a moist cotton ball to clean any discharge from the eye. Avoid putting anything irritating around, or into your dog's eyes.

Brushing teeth - Pick up a specially designed canine tooth brush and cleaning paste. Clean your dog's teeth as frequently as daily. Try to brush your dog's teeth a few times a week at a minimum. If your dog wants no part of having his or her teeth brushed, try rubbing his teeth and gums with your finger. After he is comfortable with this, you can now put some paste on your finger, allowing him to smell and lick it, then repeat rubbing his teeth and gums with your finger. Now that he is comfortable with your finger, repeat with the brush. In addition, it is important to keep plenty of chews around to promote the oral health of your pooch. When your dog is 2-3 years old, he or she may need their first professional teeth cleaning. Dogs such as Chihuahua's are notorious for having poor teeth and require frequent attention.

Anal sacs - These sacs are located on each side of a dog's anus. If you notice your dog scooting his rear, or frequently licking and biting at his anus, the anal sacs may be impacted. You can ask your veterinarian how to diagnose and treat this issue.

Doing Things: Fun and Educational

- To avoid doggy boredom, make sure you have plenty of toys for your dog to choose from out of the toy bin. A Nylabone™, a Kong™, dog chews, ropes, balls, and tugs are many of the popular things your dog can enjoy. Your more advanced breeds might enjoy mahjong, air hockey, or play station. Please limit their time playing video games.

Be sure your dog is:

- Comfortable with human male and female adults.

- Comfortable with human male and female children.

- Comfortable with special circumstance people, for example, those in wheel chairs, with crutches, braces, or even strange "Uncle Larry."

To assure that your dog isn't selfish, make sure that he or she is:

- Comfortable with sharing his food bowl, toys or bed being touched by you or others.

- Comfortable sharing the immediate space with strangers, especially with children. This is necessary for your puppy's socialization so that he doesn't get paranoid or freak out in small places. For example, elevators in Hollywood filled with celebrities and their handbags, or next-door neighbor's house.

- Comfortable sharing his best friend, YOU, and all family members and friends.

For road trippn' with your dog, make sure he or she is:

- Comfortable in a car, truck, minivan, or in a form of public transportation.

- Always properly restrained.

- Knows how to operate a stick shift as well as an automatic.

In general, a happy puppy should have the following:

- You should provide at least 10 hours of sleep per night for your dog. This should occur in one of the household's adult bedrooms, but not in your bed. He or she should have their own bed or mat available to them.

- Regular health checks at the vet are essential. He or she should receive at least the basic vaccinations, which includes rabies and distemper. Read up before agreeing on extra vaccinations and avoid unnecessary vaccinations or parasite treatments.

- Unless you are going to breed your dog, it is necessary that they be neutered or spayed.

- Maintain a proper weight for your dog. You should be able to feel his ribs but they do not stick out. He or she will have their weight checked at the vet and this will inform you on your dog's optimal weight.

- Plenty of play-time outside with proper supervision.

- It is essential that your dog have daily long walks, play, sport, or games.

Dog First Aid Kit Supplies

Dogs are prone to accidents and injuries and it never hurts to have a first aid kit handy. I grew up camping and hiking and my family always had a kit for us humans as well as our dogs. Whether you are an urban or rural dweller, it is always a good idea to be prepared for any mishap that might harm your dog. You will notice that many of these items listed are the same for our first aid kits, but there are some extra dog specific items that will help you in an emergency help your dog. Think about sharp rocks, insect bites, animal bites, thorns, glass, and similar items that might need tending to while you are away from the house.

Some suggested **Pet First Aid Kit Items** are Saline solution, Cotton balls and swabs, Scissors, Tweezers, Sterile gauze pads and bandages, First aid tape, Antibacterial ointment, Hydrogen peroxide, Rubbing alcohol, Antiseptic wipes, Splint, Styptic powder to stop bleeding, Sterile latex gloves, Eye wash, Benadryl for allergic reactions, Blanket, Large bottle of water, Self-activating hot and cold packs, Flash light, and Hydrocortisone cream. If you are learned in pet care then you can add some prescription medicines such as painkillers or antibiotics. Be sure to include a *muzzle, leash, and a book on pet first aid.*

Dog Nutrition

As for nutrition, humans study it, practice it, complain about it, but usually give into the science of it. Like humans, dogs have their own nutrition charts to follow, and are subject to different theories and scientific studies, as well.

In the following, we will look at the history of dog food, as well as the common sense of raw foods, nutrient lists, and what your dog might have to bark about regarding what he is ingesting.

In the beginning, there were wild packs of canines everywhere and they ate anything that they could get their paws on. Similar to human survival, dogs depended upon meat from kills, grasses, berries, and other edibles that nature provided them. Guess what the great news is? Many millennia later nature is still providing all that we need.

Some History

In history, the Romans wrote about feeding their dogs barley bread soaked in milk along with the bones of sheep. The wealthy Europeans of the 1800's would feed their dogs better food than most humans had to eat. Meat from horses and other dead animals was often rounded up from the streets to recycle as dog food for the rich estates on the outskirts of the city. Royalty is legendary for pampering their dogs with all sorts of delicacies from around the world. Meanwhile, the poor and their dogs had to fend for themselves or starve. Being fed table scraps from a pauper's diet was not sufficient to keep a dog healthy, and the humans themselves often had their own nutrition problems. To keep from starving dogs would hunt rats, rabbits, mice, and any other rodent type creature they could sink their teeth.

Other references from the 18th century tell of how the French would mix breadcrumbs with tiny pieces of meat for their dogs. It is also written that the liver, heart, blood, or all, were mixed with milk or cheese and sometimes bread was a manmade food source for domestic canine. In England, they would offer soups flavored with meat and bone to augment their dog's nutrition.

In the mid to late 1800's a middle class blossomed out of the industrial revolution. This group started taking on dogs as house pets and unwittingly created an enterprise out of feeding the household pets that were suddenly in abundance. This new class with its burgeoning wealth had extra money to spend. Noting that the sailor's biscuits kept well for long periods, James Spratt began selling his own recipe of hard biscuit for dogs in London, and shortly thereafter, he took his new product to New York City. It is believed that he single-handedly started the American dog food business. This places the dog food and kibble industry at just over 150 years old, and now is an annual multi-billion dollar business.

All the while we know that any farm dog, or for that matter, any dog that can kill something and eat it will do just that. Nothing has changed throughout the centuries. Raw meat does not kill dogs, so it is safe to say that raw food diets will not either.

Feeding Your Puppy and Adult Dog

To check if your puppy is having his proper dietary needs met, check to make sure that your puppy is active, alert, and is showing good bone and muscle development. To understand the correct portion ask the breeder to show you the portion that he or she feeds the puppies. From there observe whether your puppy is quickly devouring his food and then continuing to act as though he wants and needs more. If so, then increase the portion a little until you find the correct portion. If your puppy is eating quickly and then begins to just nibble and in the end leaves food in the bowl, then you are over-feeding your puppy. As you adjust the food portion to less or more; observe whether your puppy is gaining or losing weight so that you can find the proper portion of food to serve during feeding times. Very active puppies tend to burn lots of energy and this is one reason that a puppy might need a little extra food in his bowl. The suggested portions are on the food containers, but this is not a one-size fits all world that we live in.

Many breeders and trainers state that puppies should not leave their mothers until they are at least eight weeks old. This allows their mother's milk to boost their immunity by supporting antibodies and nutrition that is needed to become a healthy dog. Around three to four weeks old puppies should begin eating some solid food in conjunction with their mother's milk. This helps their digestion process begin to adjust to solid foods making the transition from mother's milk to their new home easier.

When choosing your puppy's feeding times, choose the times that you know will be the best for you to feed your puppy. Feeding on a regular schedule is one part of your over-all consistency that you are establishing for your puppy to know that as the alpha you are reliably satisfying their needs. After setting the feeding schedule, remain as close to those times as possible. For example, 7am, around noon, and again at 5pm. An earlier dinnertime helps your puppy to digest then eliminate before his bedtime.

Puppies are going to eat four times a day up until about eight weeks. At eight weeks, they can still be fed four times a day, or you can reduce to three times. Split the recommend daily feeding portion into thirds. Puppies' nutritional requirements differ from adult dogs so select a puppy food that has the appropriate balance of nutrients that puppies require. Puppy food should continue to support healthy growth, digestion, and the immune system. Supplying your growing puppy the correct amount of calories, protein, and calcium is part of a well-balanced diet.

During the three to six months puppy stage teething can alter your puppies eating habits. Some pups many not feel like eating due to pain, so it is your responsibility to remain diligent in your job to provide them all of their nutritional requirements and confirm that they are eating. Hint: Soaking dry food in water for 10-15 minutes before feeding will soften it and make it easier for your puppy to eat. This avoids suddenly introducing new softer foods to your puppy, and avoids the unknown consequences of doing so.

At six months to a year old, your puppy still requires high quality nutritionally charged foods. Consult your breeder or veterinarian about the right time to switch to an adult food.

When you switch to an adult food, continue to choose the highest quality food that has a specified meat, and not only by-products. Avoid unnecessary artificial additives. In many cases, the higher the quality foods that you feed your dog allows you to serve smaller portions because more of the food is being used by your dog and not just flowing through. Fillers are often not digested and this requires feeding your dog larger portions.

Additionally, follow the alpha guideline that states that *humans always eat first*. This means that the humans finish their meal entirely and clear the table before feeding their dogs, or feed your dog a couple of hours before you and your family eat. This establishes and continues the precedence that all humans are above the dog in the pecking order.

Help Identifying Dog Food Quality

- The first ingredient, or at a minimum, the second should specify *meat* or *meat meal*. NOT by-product
- **"What is a by-product?"** Unless specified on the label, a by-product can be left over parts from animals and contain parts of hooves, feet, skin, eyes, or other animal body parts.
- Beware of ingredients that use wording such as *animal* and *meat* instead of a specific word such as beef or chicken.
- "Meal" when listed in ingredients is something that has been weighed after the water was taken out, an example would be "chicken meal." This means it has been cooked with a great amount of water reduction occurring in the process, and thus it is providing more actual meat and protein per weight volume.
- As an example, if the dog food only states "beef" in the ingredients it refers to the pre-cooking weight.

This means that after cooking, less meat will be present in the food.
- A label that states "beef" first then "corn meal" secondly, is stating that the food probably contains a lot more corn than beef. Corn is not easily digested nor does it offer much in the way of nutrients that are vital to a dog's health. Furthermore, it has been linked to other health issues, and dogs are not designed to eat corn and grains in high doses. Try your best to avoid corn, wheat, and soy in your dog's food. The higher quality more expensive foods are often worth it for your dog's health.
- If you decide to change dog food formulas or brands, a gradual change over is recommended, especially if your dog has a sensitive stomach. This is done by mixing some of the old with the new and gradually increasing the amount of new throughout the week.

An example schedule of changing dog foods

Day 1-2 Mix ¼ new with ¾ old food

Day 2-4 Mix ½ new with ½ old

Day 5-6 Mix ¾ new with ¼ old

Day 7 100% of the new dog food

The Switch - Moving From Puppy to Adult Food

When your puppy is ready to make the switch from puppy to adult dog food, you can follow the same procedure above, or shorten it to a four to five day switch over. During the switch, be observant of your dog's stools and health. If your dog appears not to handle the new food formula then your options are to change the current meat to a different meat, or try a different formula or brand.

Avoid returning to the original puppy food. If you have any concerns or questions, consult your veterinarian.

Raw Food Stuff

Let us take a look-see at the raw food diet for canines. First, remember that our dogs, pals, best friends, comedy actors, were meant to eat real food such as meat. Their DNA does not only dictate them to eat dry cereals that were concocted by humans in white lab coats. These cereals based and meat-by products may have been keeping our pets alive, but possibly not thriving at optimum levels.

There are many arguments for the benefits of real and raw foods. Sure it is more work, but isn't their health worth it? It is normal, not abnormal to be feeding your dog, a living food diet; it is thought that it will greatly boost their immune system and over-all health. *All foods,* dry, wet, or raw contain a risk, as they can all contain contaminants and parasites.

There are different types of raw food diets. There are raw meats that you can prepare at home by freeze-drying or freezing that you can easily thaw to feed your dog.

Raw food diets amount to foods that are not cooked or sent through a processing plant. With some research, you can make a decision on what you think is the best type of diet for your dog. For your dog's health and for their optimal benefits it is worth the efforts of your research time to read up on a raw foods diet, or possibly a mix of kibble and raw foods.

Rules of thumb to follow for a raw food diet

1. Before switching, make sure your dog has a healthy gastro-intestinal track.

2. Be smart and do not leave meat un-refrigerated for lengthy periods.

3. To be safe, simply follow human protocol for food safety. Toss out the smelly, slimy, or the meat and other food items that just do not seem right.

4. Keep it balanced. Correct amount of vitamins and minerals, fiber, antioxidants, and fatty acids. Note any medical issues your dog has and possible diet correlations.

5. A gradual switch over between foods is recommended to allow their GI track to adjust. Use new foods as a treat, and then watch stools to see how your dog is adjusting.

6. Take note of the size and type of bones you throw to your dog. Not all dogs do well with real raw bones.

7. Freezing meats for three days, similar to sushi protocol, can help kill unwanted pathogens or parasites.

8. Take note about what is working and not working with your dog's food changes. Remember to be vigilant, and take note of your observations when tracking a new diet. If your dog has a healthy issue, your veterinarian will thank you for your thorough note taking.

9. Like us humans, most dogs do well with a variety of foods. There is no one-size-fits-all diet.

10. Please read up on raw foods diet before switching over, and follow all veterinary guidelines.

Human Foods for Dogs

Many human foods are safe for dogs. In reality, human and dog foods were similar for most of our coexistence. Well, maybe we wouldn't eat some of the vermin they eat, but if we were hungry enough we could.

Whether you have your dog on a raw food diet, a partial raw food diet, or manufactured dog foods, you can still treat with some human foods. Even a top quality dog food may be lacking in some nutrients your dog may need. In addition, a tasty safe human food, such as an apple can be used as a treat in training. Below is a short list of some safe human foods that you may feed your dog. Remember to proceed in moderation to see how your dog's digestive system reacts and adjusts to each different food. Always keep plenty of clean fresh drinking water available for your dog.

Short List of SAFE Human Foods for Dogs

Oatmeal

Oatmeal is a fantastic alternative human food source of grain for dogs that are allergic to wheat. Oatmeal's fiber can also be beneficial to more mature dogs. A general set of rules can be followed when feeding your dog oatmeal. Limit the serving sizes, and amount of serving times per week, be sure to serve the oatmeal fully cooked, and finally never add any sugar or additional flavoring.

Apples

REMOVE the seeds. Apples are an excellent human food safe for dogs to crunch on. My dog loves to munch on apples. Apples offer small amounts of both vitamin C and Vitamin A. They are a good source of fiber for a dog of any age. Caution! Do not let your dog eat the seeds of the apple OR the core as they are known to contain minute amounts of cyanide. A few will not be detrimental, so do not freak out if it happens. Just be cautious and avoid the core and seeds when treating.

Brewer's Yeast

This powder has a tangy taste that dogs will clamber over. The yeast is rich in B vitamins, which are great for the dog's skin, nails, ears, and coat. Do not confuse this with 'baking yeast,' which can make your dog ill if eaten. All you need to do is add a couple of sprinkles of brewer's yeast on your dog's food to spice it up. Most dogs really enjoy this stuff.

Brewer's yeast is made from a one-celled fungus called Saccharomyces cerevisiae and is used to make beer. Brewer's yeast is a rich source of minerals, particularly chromium, which is an essential trace mineral that helps the body maintain normal blood sugar levels, selenium, protein, and the B-complex vitamins. Brewer's yeast has been used for years as a nutritional supplement.

Eggs

Does your dog need a protein boost? Eggs are a super supplemental food because they contain ample amounts of protein; selenium, riboflavin, and they are also easily digested by your dog. Cook eggs before serving them to your best buddy, because the cooking process makes more protein available, and it make them more digestible. Eggs are good for energy, strength, and great for training as well.

Green Beans

A lean dog is a happier, more energetic dog. Feeding your dog, cooked green beans is a good source of manganese, and the vitamins C and K, additionally is they are considered a good source of fiber. If you have a lazier dog, living *"A Dog's Life,"* then it is good to be proactive with your dog's weight. Add a steady stream of fresh green beans in your dog's diet for all the right reasons. Avoid salt.

Sweet Potatoes

Vitamin C, B-6, manganese, beta-carotene, and fiber can be found in sweet potatoes. Slice them up and dehydrate and you have just found a great new healthy source for treating your dog. Next time you are out shopping for potatoes, pick up sweet potatoes, and see if your best little buddy takes to them. My bet is that your dog will love them.

Pumpkins

Pumpkins are a fantastic source of vitamin A, fiber, and beta-carotene. Trend towards a healthy diet with plenty of fiber and all the essential vitamins and proteins your dog needs. Pumpkin is one way to help you mix it up a bit. Feed it dried or moist, separate as a treat, or with his favorite foods. Pumpkin can be a fantastic, fun, and natural alternative food for dogs.

Salmon

A great source of omega 3 fatty acids, salmon is an excellent food that can support your dog's immune system, as well as his skin, coat, and overall health. Some dog owners notice when adding salmon to their dog's diet that it increases resistance to allergies. Be sure to cook the salmon before serving it. You can use salmon oil too. For treats, added flavoring to a meal, or as a complete meal, salmon is a fantastic source of natural, real food that is safe for dogs.

Flax Seed

Grounded or in oil form, flax seed is a nourishing source of omega 3 fatty acids. Omega 3 fatty acids are essential in helping your dog maintain good skin and a shiny healthy coat. Note; you will want to serve the flax seed directly after grinding it because this type of fatty acid can turn sour soon after. Flax seed is also a wonderful source of fiber your dog or puppy needs.

Yogurt

Always a great source for your dog's calcium and protein, yogurt is another one of our top ten human foods safe for dogs. Pick a fat free yogurt with no added sweeteners, or artificial sugar, color, or flavoring.

Melons

Additionally, watermelons, cantaloupes, honeydews are good for your dog. Without prior research, avoid any exotic melons or fruits.

Peanut butter

Yep, a big spoon full and it will keep him occupied for a while.

Berries (fresh & frozen)

Blueberries, blackberries, strawberries, huckleberries or raspberries provide an easy and tasty snack.

Cooked chicken

Chicken sliced up is a favorite yummy snack for your canine to enjoy in addition, or in place of his regular meal.

Beef and Beef Jerky

Jerky is a great high-value treating item for training, and beef is can be a healthy addition to your dog's diet.

Cheese

Sliced or cubed pieces are great for training or in the place of food. A tablespoon of cottage cheese on top of your dog's food will certainly be a healthy hit. Try using string cheese as a training treat.

Bananas

All fruits have phytonutrients, and other required nutrients that are essential to your canine's health.

Carrots

Crunchy veggies are good for the teeth. Carrots are full of fiber and vitamin A.

UNSAFE Human Foods

Below is a list of harmful foods for dogs. This is not a complete list, but a common list of foods known to be harmful to our canine friends. If you are unsure of a food that you wish to add to your dog's diet, please consult a veterinarian or expert on dog nutrition.

Onions: Both onions and garlic contain the toxic ingredient thiosulphate. However, onions are more dangerous than garlic because of this toxin. Many dog biscuits contain *trace* amounts of garlic, and because of this small amount, there is no threat to the health of your dog. This poison can be toxic in one large dose, or with repeated consumption that builds to the toxic level in the dog's blood.

Chocolate: Contains theobromine, a compound that is a cardiac stimulant and a diuretic. This can be fatal to dogs.

Grapes: Contains an unknown toxin that can affect kidney, and in large enough amounts can cause acute kidney failure.

Raisins: (Same as above)

Most Fruit Pits and Seeds: Contains cyanogenic glycosides, which if consumed can cause cyanide poisoning. The fruits by themselves are okay to consume.

Macadamia Nuts: Contains an unknown toxin that can be fatal to dogs.

Most Bones: Should not be given (especially chicken bones) because they can splinter and cause a laceration of the digestive system or pose a choking hazard because of the possibility for them to become lodged in your pet's throat.

Potato Peelings and Green Potatoes: Contains oxalates, which can affect the digestive, nervous, and urinary systems.

Rhubarb leaves: Contains high amount of oxalates.

Broccoli: Broccoli should be avoided, though it is only dangerous in large amounts.

Green parts of tomatoes: Contains oxalates, which can affect the digestive, nervous, and urinary systems.

Yeast dough: Can produce gas and swell in your pet's stomach and intestines, possibly leading to a rupture of the digestive system.

Coffee and tea: (due to the caffeine)

Alcoholic Beverages: Alcohol is very toxic to dogs and can lead to coma or even death.

Human Vitamins: Vitamins containing iron are especially dangerous. These vitamins can cause damage to the lining of the digestive system, the kidneys, and liver.

Moldy or spoiled foods: There are many possible harmful outcomes from spoiled foods.

Persimmons: These can cause intestinal blockage.

Raw Eggs: Salmonella.

Salt: In large doses can cause an electrolyte imbalance.

Mushrooms: Can cause liver and kidney damage.

Avocados: Avocado leaves; fruit, seeds, and bark contain a toxin known as persin. The Guatemalan variety that is commonly found in stores appears to be the most problematic. Avocados are known to cause respiratory distress in other animals, but causes less harmful problems in dogs. It is best to avoid feeding them to your dog.

Xylitol: This artificial sweetener is not healthy for dogs.

According to nutritional scientists and veterinarian health professionals, your dog needs twenty Amino Acids, and ten of which are essential. At least thirty-six nutrients and a couple of extra may be needed to combat certain afflictions. Your dog's health depends upon the intake of the following nutrients. Read labels and literature to take stock of the foods you provide.

36 Nutrients for dogs:

1. 10 essential Amino Acids – Arginine, Histidine, Isoleucine, Leucine, Lysine, Methionine. Along with Phenylalanine, Threonine, Tryptophan, and Valine.

2. 11 vitamins – A, D, E, B1, B3, B5, B6, B12, Folic Acid, and Choline.

3. 12 minerals – Calcium, Phosphorus, Potassium, Sodium, Chloride, Magnesium, Copper, Manganese, Zinc, Iodine, and Selenium

4. Fat – Linoleic Acid

5. Omega 6 Fatty Acid

6. Protein

Suggested Daily Quantities of Recommended Nutrients

Nutritient	Puppies	Adult Dogs
Protein (%)	22.0	18.0
Arginine (%)	0.62	0.51
Histidine (%)	0.22	0.18
Isoleucine (%)	0.45	0.37
Leucine (%)	0.72	0.59
Lysine (%)	0.77	0.63
Methionine + cystine (%)	0.53	0.43
Phenylalanine + tyrosine (%)	0.89	0.73
Threonine (%)	0.58	0.48
Tryptophan (%)	0.20	0.16
Valine (%)	0.48	0.39
Fat (%)	8.0	5.0
Calcium (%)	1.0	0.6
Phosphorus (%)	0.8	0.5
Sodium (%)	0.3	0.06
Chloride (%)	0.45	0.09

We realize it may take time to understand what kind of diet your dog will thrive. Do your best to include in your dog's daily diet, all thirty-six nutrients mentioned here. All of which can come from fruits, veggies, kibble, raw foods, and yes, even good table scraps. You will soon discover that your dog has preferred foods. For your dog to maintain optimum health, he needs a daily basis of a GI track healthy, well-rounded diet with a good balance of exercise, rest, socializing, care, and love.

The End is Only the Beginning

I am confident that after using this guide, you will not only be more knowledgeable about puppies and their behaviors, but your confidence and skills as a trainer will shine brightly. I hope that you have taken advantage of the free information offered in the *New Dog Starter Guide*. *No?* Then click here, and you can download it *FREE* and begin using it today.

Without a doubt, there is much more you can learn about your own dog and about the species as a whole. I am sure that you had experienced days when your dog tested your patience, and even times when you perhaps questioned your dog's intelligence, only to find that it was your perception that was wrong, and that *you were likely at fault*. No worries. This is a common occurrence, and it will likely continue with some frequency throughout your relationship together. We humans are obviously fallible, and as such, you are going to make mistakes again in the future.

Thank goodness, dogs are such forgiving animals. Whatever difficult times have transpired, I hope that you were able to work through it, and as a result, you and your dog now have a greater understanding and love of each other. The most important thing is that you have developed a command over your dog that will continuously prove itself a valuable asset into the future.

For me, befriending my dogs has proven to be an adventure, and commitment that continues to be rewarding on every level. It seems as though many times my dog Jake knows what I am thinking and acts accordingly. He invariably responds in such a way that indicates a greater understanding of me than I ever thought possible. Through the good and bad times, he always makes me smile. Even when he is at his orneriest, I get the biggest kick out of him. He is such a foolhardy, loveable, intelligent, and clownish dog, how could I be upset, or annoyed by him?

Having patience with your dog, as well as with yourself is vital. If you do this right, you will have a wonderful relationship and a deep bond that will last for years. The companionship of a dog cannot only bring joy and friendship, but can improve your health and wellbeing, as well.

Remember, dog ownership requires you to be proactive and fully engaged in your responsibility as the alpha. Given this responsibility, it is up to you to utilize other resources, such as training books, videos, and professionals, as well as other experienced dog owners who can impart to you their successes and failures. Take advantage of accessing other free guides that I will regularly be making available in support of dog training and ownership. These will be available in my newdogtimes.com website. Never stop broadening your training skills and canine knowledge. Your efforts will serve to keep you and your Airedale Terrier happy and healthy for a long, long time.

On behalf of Tom, the Pearce families and myself, I would like to thank you for reading this training guide. We thank you for visiting our blog, and downloading the free offers available on our website. Please share your new knowledge with others, as it ultimately benefits the bond between human and dog.

I hope that you have enjoyed this guide as much as I have enjoyed writing it. If this training guide informed how to train your dog, please take the time to review this guide and tell others about the positive information that you found inside. We rely on you to help us tell others about the importance of proper training, and respectful dog ownership.

Finally, I am always striving to improve both my writing and training skills, so I look forward to reading your helpful comments and insightful suggestions.

~ Paps

3 BONUS TRICKS
Teaching the "Touch" & "Release" Commands
And How to Learn Names

Excerpted from the book "49 ½ Dog Tricks"
By Paul Allen Pearce
Available in 2015

Introduction

Did you ever want to amaze and entertain your friends and family with the type of dog that can, will, and wants to do anything at any time, a show-off dog? You know that dog that understands vocal and body signals, reacts when commanded, and is a great companion in life. The tricks inside this book are the kind of fun and useful tricks that can give you that kind of dog when together you master them. After training these tricks included inside this book, you and your dog can have a joyful and fruitful life together as friends and partners in showmanship.

Health Insurance for my Dog?
Really? Why?

Because Paying Cash Makes No "Cents" or Does It?
Shocking Statistics! Discover the Truth!

healthypaws
PET INSURANCE & FOUNDATION

Protect Your Pet.
Save a Homeless Pet.

TRUSTED BY PET PARENTS & LOVED BY PETS!

Protect your best friend and save on vet bills!

- ☑ Lifetime discounts up to 10%
- ☑ Unlimited Benefits
- ☑ #1 Customer-Rated Plan

Quote and Save

CLICK FOR A FREE QUOTE NOW

OR ~ Type Into Your Browser
http://nobrainerdogtrainer.com/insurance-for-dogs/

Trick #14 Teaching Release

Release has an easy rating and requires that your dog knows the sit and stay commands. The supplies needed are your clicker, and some treats.

I use "rise" to release my dog Jake, but there is nothing wrong with using *release, move, break,* or a simple word that you feel comfortable using. Try to avoid yes, okay, and other commonly used words that are used in everyday conversation.

This command informs your dog that they are free to move from whichever previous command you had issued and your dog complied, such as *sit, down,* or *stay.* It does not imply that your dog is free to run off and play on his own. It is specifically for your dog to stand up and prepare for the next command.

Release is easier to train if your dog already *sits* and *stays* on command. If you have told your dog to stay, he will sit patiently and he should remain in the sitting position until released. This is an obedience command that can keep your dog safe and you from worrying about your dog bolting off or moving at the wrong time, and it is an easy way to let your dog know when it is acceptable for him to move.

The goals for your dog to learn are that other movements besides the release cues are not a cue to move, your dog gets up or moves immediately when you command, and your dog stays put until the command *release* is given, and besides standing up, your dog does no other actions. When successfully trained your dog will ignore all other movements and words and will release only when the proper vocal or hand signal is used.

If your dog gets up *without* the release command, *do not* click and treat. When your dog regularly obeys release, you will have greater control over your dog. This reinforces that you are the leader and in control at all times.

Do not move forward to the next step until your dog is regularly obeying the step that you are working.

1. Begin training in a quiet place with few distractions, and bring plenty of treats.

2. Select a hand signal that is not associated with another command, and that you will use in conjunction with the vocal command "release."

3. Say the command "down" to your dog. After he obeys and is in the down position, give an internal count of around three seconds, when the time is up; simultaneously issue the vocal command "release" and your hand signal. If your dog does not rise put some enthusiasm into your voice and hand signal and your dog should release, then when he does, *click and treat*. Then directly afterward command your dog back into the down position and C/T. Continue repeating until your dog upon command is regularly releasing from the down position. Gradually increase the time between the *down* command and *release* command from three to ten seconds. Repeat 6-10 times per session depending upon your dog's attention.

4. After using the excited voice and hand gesture, we will move to the vocal command and hand gesture but this time begin gradually decreasing your enthusiasm and moving towards using your normal command tone voice. Give an internal count of around ten seconds, when the time is up; simultaneously issue the vocal command "release" with your hand signal, C/T when he does. Then directly afterward command your dog back into the down position and C/T. Continue repeating until your dog upon command is regularly releasing from the down position. Repeat 6-10 times per session. Continue practicing until your dog will release when you use your normal command voice without elaborate enthusiasm or excess gestures.

5. Next, cease using the hand gesture and only use your vocal command saying "release," and when your dog does, C/T. As you practice, gradually put less enthusiasm into your voice command until you arrive at your normal command voice. Start by issuing the command "down," count off five seconds and then use only the vocal command when releasing. Then directly afterward command your dog back into the down position and C/T. Continue repeating until your dog upon command is regularly releasing from the down position. Before moving to step six, gradually increase the down-release time to 10-15 seconds. Repeat 6-10 times per session.

6. Practice the release command from the sit and down positions. Later, increase the time between your commands sit, down, stay, and issuing the release command. You want your dog to feel relaxed and good about waiting to move, and follow your next command. Increase the time that your dog stays using increments of three to five seconds per session, and when your dog becomes used to staying for longer, you can increase the increments to whatever time you and your dog are comfortable. Eventually you want to arrive at the place where your dog will stay for fifteen minutes or longer.

During the time increment increases, also increase the distance between you and your dog while your dog is in the down position. Gradually begin moving further away from your dog before issuing the vocal release command.

Go to where your dog has risen and C/T where he is standing, do not have him come to you for the treat.

7. Next, practice this in a variety of areas and in situations of various distraction. After success indoors and outdoors in your yard, then wander into the neighborhood, and beyond. Remain patient in the more distracting locations and gradually increase the amount and types of distractions. Distractions can also include his toys be tossed or played with.

- Check how your dog reacts when you grab his favorite ball or tug. Does he stay in place or rise up to play? He should remain in the down position that you had him commanded.

- If other distractions are occurring and your dog stays in the down position, give your dog a C/T for remaining down. If you notice that your dog is restless due to surrounding distractions, give a C/T while the distraction is occurring and after the distraction has ended. These reward reinforcements will help your dog understand that he is being rewarded for remaining in the positon that you requested.

- Mix up the treats and time increments so that your dog never knows when the reward or which treat is coming next.

Gradually phase out clicking and treating your dog every time that he obeys the release command. Reduce the treats to one time out of two compliances, followed by one out of three, then one out of four, five, six, and finally stop altogether. Do not decrease the treats too rapidly and be sure to observe closely, your dog's abilities and pace. The goal of the training is to have your dog obey *all* commands with only a vocal or physical cue, *without a reward.*

Hands On

The release that I taught Jake was "rise" Whenever I said "rise" Jake knew that he was free to stand up from the previous command *down*. Additionally, I use this command daily to keep him sharp. It is useful when I need him still for just a few minutes or longer while I do something. It also helps me when I want Jake to standby while I open the truck door. I say "sit," then when I am ready "rise," followed by "up" and he jumps into the truck.

Troubleshooting

My dog has ZERO patience and releases on his own clock!

This is shared with all dogs until they get used to the command. Your dog may be anticipating the count between the "down" command and the release, a solution to this is to change up the time between the command and release, such as four seconds then seven seconds the next. Another thing that humans do is give physical cues that they are not aware. A simple raised eyebrow or slight hand movement maybe triggering a perceptive dog to release. Later these other cures will gradually be trained away, so that your dog will only obey the release vocal or hand cue.

Hint: Always remain positive and excited. This will help your dog learn this trick. In training, we have to keep our frustrations hidden from dogs. Vocal, facial, physical movements and tones need to remain consistent during training. If you are frustrated or tired, finish the session on a high note and start again later or another day. There is no hurry for you or your dog to learn tricks.

Trick #10 Teaching "Touch"

Touch has an easy rating and requires no knowledge of other tricks, but your dog should know its name. The supplies needed are a wooden dowel to be used as a touch stick, your clicker, and some treats.

Touch training teaches your dog to touch, and in this lesson to touch the end of a stick. It can be any type of wooden dowel, cut broom handle, or similar that is around three feet (.9 meters) in length. During training, add a plastic cap, rubber ball, or good ole duct tape to the end so that there are no sharp edges that can harm your dog. A good sanding will also cure the problem of rough or sharp edges.

Teaching "touch" using the *touch stick* will enable you to train other tricks. You will discover that the *touch stick* is useful in training, so take care that you correctly train your dog the *touch* command. **Touch is used later to teach Learn Names, Ring Bell, Jump Over People, Spin, Jump, and more.**

1. To begin, have your dog in the sitting position or standing near you and giving his attention towards you. Hold your stick away from your body. Keep holding it while doing nothing else but holding the stick steady at a level that your dog can easily touch it with his nose.

2. Luckily, dog's natural curiosity will get the best of them and your dog should touch the stick. When your dog touches it with his nose or mouth, *click and treat*. Be sure to click immediately when your dog touches the end of the stick. Sometimes it is just a sniff, but those count for beginning to shape the command.

If your dog is not interested then you will need to do the touching for him. Do this by gently touching your dog's nose while simultaneously clicking and then treating. Keep doing this until your dog is regularly touching the stick when you hold it out.

3. The next time your dog touches the stick C/T while simultaneously saying the command, "touch." Remember timing is important in all tricks. Your dog needs to know the exact action that is the correct action, which he is being rewarded for performing. Repeat this a dozen times. Continue over multiple sessions until your dog upon command of "touch," is easily touching the end of the touch stick. Feel free to add some "good dog" praises.

Hands On

Teaching Jake this trick was an interesting outing. When I first held out the stick, Jake swiped it away with his paw. After a couple of more times, he finally smelled the end with his nose and I quickly clicked and treated. He responded quickly to that, and after reinforcing that with several more *click and treats*, he started quickly touching the end of the stick.

After using the *touch* command a dozen times, he realized a treat came after he touched the end of the stick, and moving forward through a few training sessions, he started touching it each time I issued my "touch" command. I kept practicing and after a couple of more sessions, I locked it in with Jake. I was then able to use the "touch" command and touch stick to train other tricks.

If your dog is coming in hard to touch the stick, you can add some foam to the end of the stick to cushion his *super-nose*.

Troubleshooting

What if my dog is touching the middle of the stick, or not touching the stick at all?

I mentioned that Jake took a few swipes at the end of the stick before touching it. Each time he did this, I ignored this behavior even though he looked at me expecting a reward. He could smell the treats in my hand, but I did not click and reward the wrong action. Finally, as I held the stick out close to his snout, he smelled it with his nose and I quickly clicked and treated.

Do not reward until your dog is touching *only* the end of the stick. This allows you to use the touch command in training other tricks. If your dog will not touch it try gently touching the end of the stick to his nose and C/T, but quickly move away from that and let your dog begin to do the touching on his own.

"49 ½ Dog Tricks"
By Paul Allen Pearce
Will be available in late 2015

Trick #15 Teaching to Learn Names

Learning names has an intermediate to difficult rating and requires knowledge of the touch command. The supplies needed are a toy, treats, and your clicker.

Dog owners have known for years that dogs are smarter than many people give them credit. They are capable of learning the names of many different objects such as their toys, people, and places such as rooms. Using the steps in this exercise your dog can learn the names of all your family members, his personal items such as his crate, collar, and leash. Beyond those items, your dog can learn the names of different rooms, which enable you to use the "go" command to have your dog, go to a specific room. Dogs have been known to learn hundreds and even upwards to a thousand words. Furthermore, once your dog learns the name of something, he or she can find it, take it, and bring it to you.

Not all dogs are capable of learning the same number of words and some will learn and retain better than others, so do not get frustrated if it takes some time for your dog to recognize and remember what object, place, or person goes with the name you are speaking. Select a toy that you may already refer to by name. Chances are that you already often speak the names of dog-associated items when speaking to your dog and he recognizes that word. Be consistent in your name references to your dog's toys such as Frisbee™, tug, ball, rope, and squeaky.

1. To begin, find a low distraction area, treats at the ready, and one of your dog's favorite toys. I will use *tug* in this example.

2. Start by using *touch* and have your dog touch your empty hand, when he does, *click and treat* your dog. Repeat this five times.

3. Next, grab your dog's toy into your hand, say, "touch," and if he touches the tug and not your hand, C/T your dog.

4. Repeat number three, but this time, add the toy name, say, "touch tug." When your dog touches the *tug*, and nothing else, C/T at that exact moment he does this. Repeat this 6-10 times.

5. After a break, practice steps 1-4 over a few sessions, and a day or two.

6. In the next phase warm up with numbers 1-4, then hold the tug out away from you and say "touch tug," when he does C/T. Repeat this 6-10 times. Then extend the tug at full arm lengths from you and repeat 6-10 times. Practice this over a couple of sessions. Take note of your dog's progress and when he is ready, proceed to number seven.

7. Now, place the tug onto the floor but keep your hand on it, and say, "touch tug," when he does, C/T. Repeat 6-10 times.

8. Now, place it on the floor without your hand upon it, and say, "touch tug," and when he does, treat a barnbuster sized treat serving. Feel free to throw in some verbal good boy/girls. If your dog is not moving to it, be patient, silent, and still, and see if he can figure it out on his own. Remember that your dog wants his treat.

9. Moving forward with the same toy, place it around the room in different areas, increasingly further from you. Place it on top of a small stool, on the ground, and or low-lying shelves and have your dog "touch tug." Practice this over a few days and when your dog is regularly responding move onto number ten and a new toy.

10. Move onto another toy. Use a toy such as Frisbee™ that when said sounds much different when the word is spoken than the previous toy name. Repeat the steps 4-9 with this next toy.

11. Time to test if your dog can tell the difference. Sit down on the couch or floor and place both the Frisbee™ and the tug behind you. Take out the Frisbee and practice five touches, C/T each time your dog correctly touches upon command. Next, do the same with the tug.

12. Now, hold one toy in each hand and say, "touch Frisbee™" and see if your dog touches the correct toy. If your dog touches the Frisbee™, C/T, and give a barnbuster sized reward. If your dog begins to move towards the Frisbee™, but you see that he is unsure, C/T him for moving in the correct direction. If your dog goes to the tug or does nothing, remain neutral offering no C/T or verbal reward.

Keep working on this and practicing until your dog regularly goes to the correct toy that you command to be touched. Then following the same process continue adding toys. When you get to three, then four, toys/objects you can lay out all four in front of you and command "touch (object name)" and see if your dog can choose and recognize the correct toy/object.

13. Practice the "touch tug, ball, Frisbee, chew" by placing the objects in different parts of the room and have him identify each correctly. Practice this often to keep the names fresh in your dog's mind.

14. Teaching names of people is done a little differently, because for obvious reasons you cannot hold them in your hand, if they are willing, you could however have them sit on the floor. Trick #8 "Train Your Dog to Go To a Place" will teach you how to use the training stick to help train the names of rooms and things such as crate, bed, and mat. You can use the training stick to introduce the person.

Alternative to #14 above - Teaching a person's name to your dog can be taught like this.

1. Hold onto your dog's collar and have a family member show your dog a treat. Have the person walk into the other room. Then say, "Jake, find Michelle," or whatever the person's name is. Now let go of the collar and see if your dog will go into the other room and to that person. It is okay to follow your dog. If he does go to the person, give your dog a C/T and a huge barnbuster reward along with praise.

2. Repeat five times and take a break.

3. After number two, have the family member go into different rooms, and do five repetitions in each room.

4. It will take a few sessions for your dog to learn and retain the names. Do not forget to reinforce practicing forever.

Hands On

I taught this to Jake, but my wife's Poodle Roxie knows many more names of objects, people, and places, but Jake can respectably perform all of the tricks in here. He is my pal and goes through all of these things willingly, but some days I have to give him a break, probably like crash test dummies in the car industry need a break.

Teaching Jake names while using the "touch" command I started out by using the touch command with my empty hand, and getting a peculiar look from him. He touched my hand and I C/T about a half dozen times. Holding Jakes attention while in the sitting position in front of me, I then I picked up the tug into my hand and repeated the exercise saying, "touch tug," and only C/T when he touched the tug. I'll confess it took a few attempts and me adjusting my hand so that he had to touch the tug when he moved his nose towards my hand holding the tug. I ran through exercises 1-4 over a few days and about six sessions.

Eventually, I felt confident to start moving the tug further from my body and then onto the floor, couch cushion, into the corner of the room and so forth. It took some time and patience for him to begin to understand right away to go to the item being named. Eventually, I was able to place it into different rooms inside the house and call out "touch tug" and he would bolt off looking for it. From there I added further toys such as Frisbee™, which I discovered by his ears and the way that he looked at me when I said the word that he already recognized the sound of the word.

Troubleshooting

I am scratching my head because my dog does not understand what I am trying to teach!

In the beginning, you can try maneuvering your hand so that your dog will touch the toy and not your hand.

Watch your time when training. Keep your sessions short and if your dog is still a puppy or acting like one keep your sessions around 3-5 minutes, while older dogs can go about 10 minutes per training session. If you notice any signs of fatigue, end the session on a high, happy note, and stop for the day and begin anew the following day.

Hint: After your dog recognizes, and is regularly touching objects in different locations, solicit other people to practice giving your dog the command. Combine this with "take it" & "bring it" and your dog will go find and bring to you anything he has learned the name. Have fun and enjoy adding objects and names.

...This book contains fun tricks as well as other useful tricks that all dogs should know that would benefit them and their owners. When your dog learns and masters all 49 ½ tricks, you will have a well-mannered, obedient, talented dog that is your friend, show-off, and companion. You two will be sure to get plenty of laughs and applause by combining these fun tricks and utilitarian commands.

I wrote this to help dog owners and trainers further their dog's abilities and the bond between dog and owner...

"49 ½ Dog Tricks"
By Paul Allen Pearce
Will be available in late 2015

If this training guide informed how to train your dog, please take the time to REVIEW this guide and tell others about the positive information inside.

I CAN'T PAY POOP!
BUT 'YOU' CAN...

Pay it Forward!
Right? Pretty Please?
REVIEW-ME

http://www.amazon.com/Paul-Allen-Pearce/e/B00HXF31C4

DON'T THiNK – BE, ALPHA DOG

I wrote this book to inform and instruct dog owners of the fundamentals for establishing and maintaining the *alpha* position within the household hierarchy. Inside the book you will learn how to live, lead, train, and love your dog in a **non-physical alpha dog way**. Leading from the *alpha* position makes everything dog related *easier*. All dogs need to know where they are positioned within the family (pack), and to understand, and trust that their *alpha* will provide food, shelter, guidance, and affection towards them. Then life becomes *easier* for you and your dog.

Whether or not you have read one of my "No Brainer Dog Trainer..." breed specific training books, I am confident that this guide will assist you while you train your dog companion. With these *alpha* fundamentals, your dog will obey your commands in critical situations, and follow your lead into a safer and happier life. Remember, having an obedient dog keeps other animals and humans safe.

A dog that respects his *alpha* leader is easier to control, teach, and trust. He is more likely to obey your commands and respect your rules. Be the *alpha* now.

~ *Paps*

"Alpha Dog Secrets" by Paul Allen Pearce
LEARN MORE:
http://www.amazon.com/dp/B00ICGQO40

Airedale Terrier Facts

Country of Origin: United Kingdom

Other Names: Waterside Terrier, Bingley Terrier

Nicknames: Aire, Airedale, King of Terriers

Group: Terrier

Purpose: Otter hunting

Size: Large

Height: Males 22 - 24 inches (56 - 61 cm) Females 22 - 23 inches (56 - 58 cm)

Weight: Males 50 - 65 pounds (23 - 29 kg) Females 40 - 45 pounds (18 - 20 kg)

Lifespan: 10-12 years

Litter Sizes: Average nine.

Colors: Black saddle with tan ears, legs, head.

Coat: Shorthaired double coat. Trim excess hair between footpads, should be plucked twice yearly, more for show dogs. Daily beard washing, burrs tend to stick.

Shedding: If kept stripped they shed little to no hair, if not they will shed even with daily brushing.

Apartment: Not recommended, highly active indoors, medium to large yard is recommended.

Temperament: Protective, courageous, friendly, intelligent, loyal, and have a strong prey drive. Aire's can do well with children if socialized early; sometimes play to rough for toddlers.

Exercise: Long daily walks, play, and or sport, they love swimming and retrieving. Important to get them exercised and avoid potential behavioral issues. For the first two years, Aire's require extra allotments of exercise.

Training: Establish yourself as the alpha and lead with confidence and firm but fair authority. Mix up your training and treats so they do not become bored. You may have to do some extra work on jumping, begin early. When beginning training find a secure, low distraction area free of any animal or human intrusions and distractions.

Notes: Watch them around small animals; it is difficult to control them when in they are in pursuit of prey.

Recognitions: ACA, ACR, AKC, ANKC, APRI, CKC, CKC, CET, DRA, FCI, KDGB, NAPR, NKC, NZKC, UKC

Airedale Terrier Rescue

Airedale Terriers are often acquired without any clear understanding of what goes into owning one, and these dogs regularly end up in the care of rescue groups, and are badly in need of adoption or fostering. If you are interested in adopting an Airedale, a rescue group is a good place to start. I have listed a few below. If you have the facilities and ability please rescue a dog and enjoy the rewarding experience that it offers both of you.

http://www.animalshelter.org/shelters/states.asp

UK -

http://www.thekennelclub.org.uk/services/public/findarescue/Default.aspx?breed=3059

http://www.airedalerescue.net/

http://www.soar-airedale-rescue.com/

https://www.aire-rescue.org/

Hey...Did I miss something?

STUMPED?

Got a Question about Your Airedale Terrier?

Ask an Expert Now!

Facebook ~

https://www.facebook.com/newdogtimes

NewDogTimes ~

http://newdogtimes.com/

It's where the **Airedale Terrier Secrets** have been hidden -since their Ancestral Wolf Packs were forced to collide with Man...

Wait Until You Learn This

ARE YOU ALPHA DOG

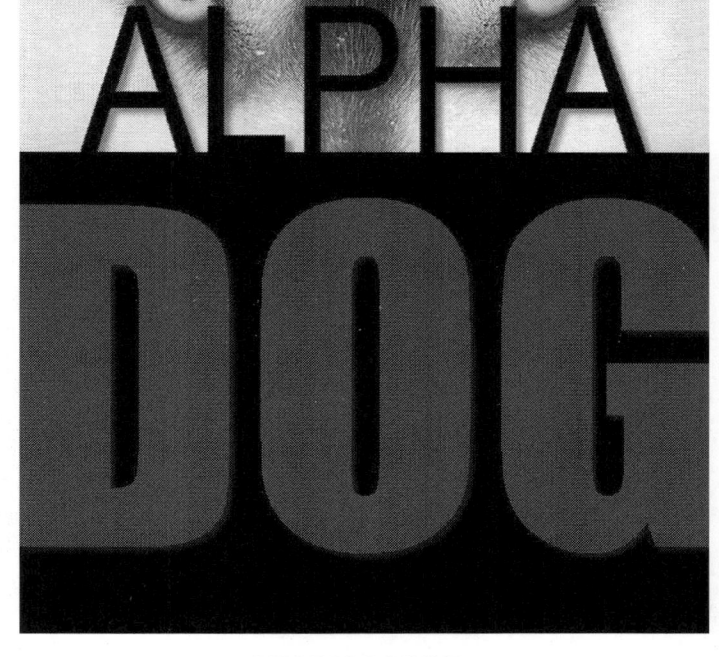

LEARN MORE:

http://www.amazon.com/dp/B00ICGQO40

About the Author

Paul Allen Pearce is the author of many breed specific dog-training books.

As a youth, a family trip to Australia forever changed the course Paul would take on his way to return home to South Carolina to begin a family, raise dogs, and eventually write. For a year in high school, Paul headed back to Australia to study, and then again, during college he did the same. After finishing college, he headed to Africa to work with the Peace Corps.

Paul's family is dog lovers and often took in strays. Paul and his siblings were taught how to care and train the family pets and dogs. Both his parents grew up with many animals and had generational knowledge to pass forth to their offspring. Being reared around all sorts of animals, his curiosity to work with animals grew. Upon returning back to the U.S. and purchasing his own dog he realized he didn't know as much as he could, thus began his journey into owning and full time dog training.

Paul states, "Dog training is my passion. I love dogs, animals, and the wonders of nature. It is easy to write about your passion and share what you have learned and discovered. I hope that my readers enjoy and learn from what I have learned and improve their dog relationships. My past explorations throughout twenty countries and states helped me to broaden my perspective regarding animal behavior and treatment. Let us all be kind to animals, not only dogs."

Visit me at NewDogTimes

Free Thank You! Gift

WAIT!

Got Yours Yet?

New Dog Training Jump Start Guide

Click to

Download Yours Here! or ▶

http://newdogtimes.com/jump-start-guide/

Other Books

"Don't Think BE, Alpha Dog Secrets Revealed"

"No Brainer Dog Trainer"
(Dog training series)

Content Attributions

Photos: We wish to thank all of the photographers for sharing their photographs via Creative Commons Licensing.

COVER
https://upload.wikimedia.org/wikipedia/commons/2/2c/Airedale_Terrier_Face.jpg, By Angela Montillon (originally posted to Flickr as beleidigt) [CC BY-SA 2.0 (http://creativecommons.org/licenses/by-sa/2.0)], via Wikimedia Commons

BIO https://upload.wikimedia.org/wikipedia/commons/a/a1/Airedale-terrier-charles14m.jpg, By Zuni1520 (Own work) [GFDL (http://www.gnu.org/copyleft/fdl.html), GFDL (http://www.gnu.org/copyleft/fdl.html) or CC BY-SA 3.0 (http://creativecommons.org/licenses/by-sa/3.0)], via Wikimedia Commons

BIO2
https://upload.wikimedia.org/wikipedia/commons/a/a3/War_Dog_Training%2C_Britain%2C_C_1940_D440.jpg, By Ministry of Information Photo Division Photographer [Public domain], via Wikimedia Commons,

PUPPY PROTOCOL
https://upload.wikimedia.org/wikipedia/commons/f/f4/01_Puppy_Airedale_Terrier.jpg, By Marilyn Peddle (Flickr: Phoebe's Pups) [CC BY 2.0 (http://creativecommons.org/licenses/by/2.0)], via Wikimedia Commons

TRAINING
https://upload.wikimedia.org/wikipedia/commons/c/c7/Troy_haven_logo.jpg, By Havenkennels (Own work) [CC BY-SA 3.0 (http://creativecommons.org/licenses/by-sa/3.0)], via Wikimedia Commons

CLICKER https://upload.wikimedia.org/wikipedia/commons/4/43/AiredaleDog.jpg, By Angela Montillon (Flickr) [CC BY-SA 2.0 (http://creativecommons.org/licenses/by-sa/2.0)], via Wikimedia Commons

TERRIER BREEDS - Photo credit: <a href="https://www.flickr.com/photos/derekskey/7184026276/">derekskey</a> / <a href="http://foter.com/">Foter</a> / <a href="http://creativecommons.org/licenses/by/2.0/">CC BY</a>, http://creativecommons.org/licenses/by/2.0/

NAME
https://upload.wikimedia.org/wikipedia/commons/1/15/Kufa_airedale_teriera.jpg, By Lilly M (za zgod? mojej znajomej - wikipedystki) [CC BY-SA 2.5 (http://creativecommons.org/licenses/by-sa/2.5)], via Wikimedia Commons

DOWN https://upload.wikimedia.org/wikipedia/commons/b/bd/Airedale_terrier.jpg, By Ioan Bodean (originally posted to Flickr as airedale terrier) [CC BY-SA 2.0 (http://creativecommons.org/licenses/by-sa/2.0)], via Wikimedia Commons

STAY "Airedale Terrier Face" by Angela Montillon - originally posted to Flickr as beleidigt. Licensed under CC BY-SA 2.0 via Wikimedia Commons - https://commons.wikimedia.org/wiki/File:Airedale_Terrier_Face.jpg#/media/File:Airedale_Terrier_Face.jpg

GO https://www.flickr.com/photos/toaireisdivine/3224318686/, CC License 2.0 Generic https://creativecommons.org/licenses/by/2.0/legalcode, Airedale Backseat Driver, Lulu Hoeller, no changes made

THE END https://www.flickr.com/photos/derekskey/7184050562/, CC License 2.0 Generic https://creativecommons.org/licenses/by/2.0/legalcode, Gus - 14, By Derek Key, cropped into Airedale
FACTS http://www.flickr.com/photos/32565072@N00/2975841150, CC License 2.0 Generic https://creativecommons.org/licenses/by/2.0/legalcode, By Jon Haynes Photography, no changes made
RESCUE
https://upload.wikimedia.org/wikipedia/commons/c/c0/When_I_grow_up_I_want_to_ be_COOL%21_fixed.JPG, By Armscliffe (Own work) [CC BY-SA 3.0 (http://creativecommons.org/licenses/by-sa/3.0) or GFDL (http://www.gnu.org/copyleft/fdl.html)], via Wikimedia Commons
JACK RUSSELL JUMPING -
http://upload.wikimedia.org/wikipedia/commons/5/55/Jack_Russell_Terrier_Lola.jpg, By Steve-65 (Own work) [CC BY-SA 3.0 (http://creativecommons.org/licenses/by-sa/3.0)], via Wikimedia Commons, no changes made
TOY MANCHESTER TERRIER agility weave
http://upload.wikimedia.org/wikipedia/commons/a/ab/Toy-manchester-terrier-weave.png, By User Coneslayer on en.wikipedia (Matthew Hunt (Coneslayer).) [CC BY-SA 2.0 (http://creativecommons.org/licenses/by-sa/2.0)], via Wikimedia Commons, no changes made
American Staffordshire Terrier_bandana -
http://upload.wikimedia.org/wikipedia/commons/d/d9/AmericanStafforshireTerrier.jpg, By GoodOlDoctorCrunk (Joey Seay) [Public domain], via Wikimedia Commons, No changes made
Leash 2 https://www.flickr.com/photos/andynash/14983873558, CC License 2.0 Generic https://creativecommons.org/licenses/by/2.0/legalcode, Bern Dog on Leash signs, Andrew Nash, no changes made
Treats - http://upload.wikimedia.org/wikipedia/commons/e/ef/Treats-IMGP9845-1.jpg,By Stacy Lynn Baum (Stacy Lynn Baum) [CC-BY-3.0 (http://creativecommons.org/licenses/by/3.0)], via Wikimedia Commons, No changes were made
Digger in action - https://www.flickr.com/photos/31064702@N05/3447086205/, CC License 2.0 https://creativecommons.org/licenses/by-sa/2.0/legalcode, taking a break, By Dawn Huczek, No changes made.
Digging Jack Russell - https://www.flickr.com/photos/ssicore/428501528, CC License 2.0, gophering, By Stephanie Sicore, No changes were made.
Body Language, Dog by dirt pile -
https://www.flickr.com/photos/31064702@N05/3447086205/, CC License 2.0 https://creativecommons.org/licenses/by-sa/2.0/legalcode, taking a break, By Dawn Huczek, No changes were made.
Basic Care & Human Goals Ear Cleaning
https://www.flickr.com/photos/dogfoto/9108187542, CC License 2.0 https://creativecommons.org/licenses/by/2.0/legalcode, Lotus, American_Staffordshire_Terrier, By Jay Lee, No changes made

Legal Disclaimer:

The author of **"No Brainer Dog Trainer" dog training books,** Paul Allen Pearce is in no way responsible at any time for the action of your pet, not now or in the future. Animals, without warning, may cause injury to humans and/or other animals. Paul Allen Pearce is not responsible for attacks, bites, mauling, nor any other viciousness or any and all other damages. We strongly recommend that you exercise caution for the safety of self, the animal, and all around the animals while working with your dog. We are not liable for any animal or human medical conditions or results obtained from training. While all attempts have been made to verify information provided in this publication, neither the author nor the publisher assume any responsibility for errors, omissions or contrary interpretation of the subject matter contained herein. The publisher and author assume no responsibility or liability whatsoever on the behalf of any purchaser or reader of the material provided. The owner of said dog training guide assumes any, and all risks associated with the methodology described inside the dog-training guidebook.

Printed in Great Britain
by Amazon.co.uk, Ltd.,
Marston Gate.